Commending the Faith

Dwight L. Moody at 45

Commending the Faith

The Preaching of D. L. Moody

Edited by

Garth Rosell

P. O. Box 3473
Peabody, Massachusetts 01961–3473

Printed in the United States of America

ISBN 1–56563–113–7

Library of Congress Cataloging-in-Publication Data

Moody, Dwight Lyman, 1837–1899.
[Selections. 1999]
Commending the faith: the preaching of D. L. Moody / [edited by] Garth M. Rosell.
Includes index.
ISBN 1–56563–113–7
1. Sermons, Evangelistic. 2. Sermons, American. I. Rosell, Garth. II. Title.
BV3797.M7S472 1999
252′.3—dc21 99–28573
CIP

for
Karen and Robert

Table of Contents

Sermons on Christian Service

Talks on Scripture and Prayer

Sermons on Heaven

Foreword

During the years of his active ministry, between 1875 and 1899, D. L. Moody preached approximately 260 different sermons. Some of these were delivered only once. Most however, like great symphonies, were preached again and again—to a variety of audiences in a number of different settings.[1]

Given Moody's enormous popularity, it is not surprising that his sermons soon found their way into print. Often transcribed by journalists, Moody's sermons were published in newspapers, magazines, and books around the world. During his lifetime alone, more than eighty different titles of his sermons and addresses appeared in print. Some of them became immediate bestsellers.

The sermons in this volume were selected primarily from the early years of Moody's ministry. Though some modern readers might be surprised by Moody's blunt and frequently colloquial style of preaching, few will remain untouched by its freshness, vitality, and persuasive power. Moody believed the gospel he proclaimed, and he wanted those who heard it to believe it too.

The fifteen sermons and sets of talks and prayers in this collection have been edited for ease of reading. The volumes from which they were taken, all published between 1875 and 1904, are listed in the table of contents so that those who wish to do so can compare the sermons in this collection with their originals. The materials are also grouped in five clusters of three in order to highlight some of the central themes in Moody's preaching.

I want especially to express my gratitude to Patrick Lowthian, who aided me in the preparation of the manuscript; to the Rev. Beth Jenkins Ernest, whose suggestion gave this project its original impetus; to the trustees, administration, and faculty of Gordon-Conwell Theological Seminary for providing the sabbatical that allowed me to prepare the materials for publication; and to the editorial staff at Hendrickson Publishers for their encouragement, professional skill, and good humor throughout the process.

As we mark the centennial of Moody's death, it seems appropriate that the voice that was so familiar to generations in the past should be heard again as we begin the new millennium.

Notes

1. Wilbur M. Smith, ed., *The Best of D. L. Moody* (Chicago: Moody, 1971), 13–15; idem, *Dwight Lyman Moody: An Annotated Bibliography* (Chicago: Moody: 1948), 105–8.

Introduction

"Some day you will read in the papers that D. L. Moody of East Northfield is dead," quipped the famous evangelist with a twinkle in his eye. "Don't you believe a word of it! At that moment I shall be more alive than I am now, I shall have gone up higher, that is all; out of this old clay tenement into a house that is immortal—a body that death cannot touch; that sin cannot taint; a body fashioned like unto his glorious body. I was born of the flesh in 1837. I was born of the Spirit in 1856. That which is born of the flesh may die. That which is born of the Spirit will live forever."[1]

Moody's death on December 22, 1899, was reported in the press. Indeed, articles appeared in literally hundreds of newspapers across America and around the world. "Dwight L. Moody Is Dead," announced the headline in the *New York Times*.[2] Those who had gathered at the graveside near the old family homestead in East Northfield, however, didn't believe a word of it. For as they watched the casket lowered into the ground—accompanied by the songs of the Northfield–Mount Hermon students and the prayers of old friends like R. A. Torrey and C. I. Scofield—they could not help but remember the remarkable words of the one whom they had gathered to honor. When I give up this "old clay tenement," Moody was certain, I "shall be more alive" than ever before, with a "body fashioned like unto his glorious body."

Although a century has now passed since Moody's mortal body was laid to rest in the gentle Massachusetts hills he so greatly loved, his memory continues to flourish in the institutions he founded, the sermons he preached, and the remarkable life he lived. Over sixty biographies,[3] hundreds of articles,[4] and scores of editions of his sermons[5] have been published since *The London Discourses* first appeared in 1875.[6] During the years of Moody's active ministry alone, between 1875 and 1899, over eighty different titles of his sermons and addresses were published. Some of these became immediate bestsellers. Sales of his sermon on *Heaven and How to Get There*, published in 1880, had reached 325,000 copies by 1900. *The Way to God*, Moody's little nine-sermon volume published in 1884, had sold 435,000 copies by the end of the century.[7]

The Early Years

Moody's popularity was enormous. Traveling in excess of a million miles, he preached in person to more than one hundred million people during his evangelistic career.[8] Born February 5, 1837, the sixth of Edwin and Betsy Moody's nine children, Dwight Lyman had not seemed destined for such greatness. Although rooted in the rich soil of New England Puritanism, the Moody family had remained poor and perennially in debt.[9] The tragic death of his father, due perhaps to "too much whiskey" as John Pollock has suggested, came when Dwight was only four.[10] His mother, then eight months pregnant and soon to have nine hungry mouths to feed (seven boys and two girls, all under the age of thirteen), was left with few resources—having lost virtually everything to the creditors but the little white clapboard farmhouse and two acres of land.[11]

Forced by these difficult circumstances to scratch out a living from the soil, Moody soon discovered that he was not cut out to be a farmer. "While cutting and hauling logs on the mountain side with his brother Edwin one day in the early spring of 1854," he exclaimed, "I'm tired of this! I'm not going to stay around here any longer. I'm going to the city."[12] So it was, as David Maas has phrased it, that the "awkward country boy with a grade-school education" made his way to Boston to find a new life and career.[13] He arrived in the big city in April, with high hopes, no job, and little cash.

Boston

Mid-nineteenth-century Boston was a thriving city of 150,000—poised on the edge of an industrial revolution and urban explosion that were destined to reshape the very contours of its geography and culture.[14] Waves of immigrants, including thousands of Irish forced from their homeland by a devastating potato famine, flooded into America's urban centers, swelling populations and competing for limited resources.[15] Moody himself, forced to live hand-to-mouth, had difficulty finding work. "I remember how I walked up and down the streets" of Boston trying to find a job, Moody later recalled. "It seemed as if there was room for every one else in the world, but none for me. I had the feeling that no one wanted me. It [was] an awful feeling."[16]

In desperation, Moody finally swallowed his pride and asked his uncle, Samuel Holton, for a job in his shoe store. Uncle Samuel, despite some hesitation about his nephew's suitability for the position, agreed to the arrangement—with the understanding that young Moody would "not try to run the store" and that he would agree to attend the Vernon Congregational Church on a regular basis. Making good on his promise, Moody enrolled as a member of the Sunday school, and was assigned to a young men's Bible class conducted by Edward Kimball.

Moody's Conversion

Unknown to Moody at the time, however, was the fact that his association with Kimball, the middle-aged teacher of his Sunday school class, was to change his life forever.[17] For while Moody was seeking his fortune in the city, the "Hound of Heaven" was seeking him—prompting Kimball to visit Moody at Holton's shoe store to "inquire about the condition of his soul." Kimball found Moody in the back of the store wrapping and shelving shoes. "I went up to him," Kimball later recalled, put "my hand on his shoulder," and "made what I afterwards felt was a very weak plea for Christ. I don't know what words I used, nor could Mr. Moody tell. I simply told him of Christ's love for him and the love Christ wanted in return. That was all there was. It seemed the young man was just ready for the light that then broke upon him and there, in the back of that store in Boston, he gave himself and his life to Christ."[18]

A modest plaque now marks the site of Holton's shoe store, long since replaced by other buildings, to commemorate this remarkable event. Inscribed are the following words: "D. L. Moody, Christian Evangelist, Friend of Man, Founder of the Northfield Schools, Was converted to God in a Shoe Store on this Site, April 21, 1855."[19] My father, Dr. Merv Rosell, was privileged to be the preacher when that event was celebrated at the Court Street site. "I was invited by an all-Boston committee to be the speaker at the centennial of D. L. Moody's conversion," Dad later recalled. "The Salvation Army band led the parade from central Boston to a special platform (high above the street) near the location of the shoe store where the famed D. L. Moody made his eternal decision. In the middle of my sermon, a boisterous 'cowboy from the west' who called himself 'Tex' mounted the steps to the pulpit area, demanding that I pray for him 'there and then.' So I carefully led this 'Bull Rider who was from the Rodeo at the Boston Garden' to prayerful faith in Christ. Then, steering him to counselors, I turned to the large, patient crowd and said, 'Now, let me give you the final point of this message.' That is how my young life was touched by Moody's conversion."[20] Moody and Kimball, I suspect, would have rejoiced.

Moody's conversion literally turned his life around. The young man with only a fourth- or fifth-grade education became the founder of three great schools.[21] The child with atrocious spelling became the catalyst for two of America's largest religious book publishers.[22] The "awkward country boy" from rural America became one of the world's most effective urban evangelists.[23] The young man who was turned down when he first applied for church membership laid the foundation for Chicago's great Moody Memorial Church and inspired the establishment of many others.[24] The boy who "thumbed through Genesis looking for the Gospel of John" became the founder of a great summer Bible conference.[25] The teenager who chopped wood on the farm became the man who preached to presidents.[26] The young man who slept on chairs at the local YMCA became that organization's president.[27] The boy brought up in poverty helped to raise tens of thousands of dollars for relief. The one some liked to call "Crazy Moody" became the one God chose to preach the gospel to more people around the world than anyone else in his generation. "The world has yet to see," British evangelist Henry Varley had once commented to Moody, "what God can do with a man fully consecrated to him." "By God's help," Moody later responded, "I aim to be that man."[28]

Chicago

More than a decade would pass following Moody's conversion before he was ready to assume the worldwide ministry with which his name is now so universally associated. A move to Chicago, his struggles with the temptations of the city, the lure of career and financial success all combined to test the resolve of the young Christian. But inspired by "Mother" Phillips, the remarkable woman who became Moody's spiritual mentor,[29] encouraged by his developing friendship with Emma C. Revell, the young woman who would later become his wife,[30] strengthened by J. B. Stillson, the Presbyterian elder who became a kind of surrogate father to Moody, helped by the generosity of John V. Farwell, whose financial support became so important to the work Moody was trying to do, and energized by the great prayer revival that swept America's urban centers in 1857 and 1858,[31] Moody began to change his focus from earning money to winning souls. "I had never lost sight of Jesus Christ since the first time I met him in the store in Boston," he later explained, "but for years I really believed that I could not work for God."

Despite these misgivings, Moody began to throw his considerable energies into Christian work.

Renting four pews in Chicago's Plymouth Congregational Church, Moody began to go out on the street to find young men to fill them. He soon started his own mission Sunday school and gradually built its attendance to over fifteen hundred students. "Still none were converted," he later admitted, since Moody was convinced that was not his task.

"Then," said Moody, "God opened my eyes." "There was a class of young ladies in the school," he explained, "who were, without exception, the most frivolous set of girls I ever met. One Sunday the teacher was ill, and I took that class. They laughed in my face, and I felt like opening the door and telling them all to go out and never come back." That week, however, "the teacher of the class came into the store where I worked. He was pale and looked very ill. 'What is the trouble?' I asked. 'I have another hemorrhage from the lungs. The doctor says I cannot live on Lake Michigan, so I am going back to New York State. I suppose I am going to die.' He seemed greatly troubled, and when I asked the reason, he replied: 'Well, I have never led any of my class to Christ. I really believe I have done the girls more harm than good.' "

"I had never heard anyone talk like that before," Moody confessed, "and it set me to thinking. After a while I said: 'Suppose you go and tell them how you feel. I will go with you.' He consented, and we started out together. It was one of the best journeys I ever had on earth. We went to the house of one of the girls, called for her, and the teacher talked to her about her soul. There was no laughing then. Tears stood in her eyes before long. After he had explained the way of life, he suggested that we have a word of prayer. He asked me to pray. True, I had never done such a thing in my life as to pray God to convert a young lady there and then. But we prayed, and God answered our prayer." Then the two men continued from house to house until every member of that little class had been converted. "I tell you," Moody later wrote, that God used that experience to kindle "a fire in my soul that has never gone out."[32]

Moody Changes Careers

That remarkable series of events in 1860 convinced Moody that he should leave his business career, seek to live on his savings, economize in every way possible (including leaving his comfortable boarding-place to sleep on the chairs in the local YMCA), and give his full attention to spreading the gospel. Moreover, his city mission work, his ministry to soldiers during the Civil War, his marriage to Emma, and his YMCA presidency were all beginning to open new opportunities for service.

Moody's ministry in England, Ireland, and Scotland, however, was what made his name a household word.[33] This ministry reached its climax between March and July of 1875. Moody and Ira Sankey (whose music came to be known and loved around the world) held eighty-five meetings and ministered to two and a half million people in

London alone. "Moody's plain, urgent message was backed by his integrity, his skill in bringing out the best in the hundreds of clergy and laity who worked with him, and by his refusal to answer critics or indulge in controversy."[34]

Over the next twenty-five years, huge crowds would gather to hear Moody and Sankey wherever they ministered; their unique approach would literally transform the understanding and practice of mass evangelism. "Moody's impact," David W. Bebbington has argued, helped to change modern revivalism "in six key ways": It was interdenominational; it involved more lay leadership than ever before; it linked the revivals with social reform; its theology emphasized human will and emotion more than reason; it stressed the importance of organizational strategy; and it helped to encourage Christians from many denominations and traditions to join hands in common cause.[35]

Moody's preaching in these great crusades, as Stanley N. Gundry has suggested, was drawn directly from the Scriptures and human experience. Moreover, his preaching was focused "on three great Bible truths"—namely, that everyone is sinful and destined for hell; that the only remedy for sin is the atoning blood of Jesus Christ; and that only the power of the Holy Spirit can bring about redemption.[36] Again and again, readers will encounter these themes in the fifteen sermons in this volume. Although they were first heard over a century ago, they remain as fresh and relevant for the reader today as they were for the first listeners.

Reasons for Moody's Appeal

His Refreshing Honesty

The reasons for Moody's enormous appeal are really quite simple. First of all, people on both sides of the Atlantic were drawn to Moody because of his refreshing honesty. When, for example, D. L. and Emma Moody first visited England in 1867, to attend the Sunday school convention that was being held in London, the vice-chairman of the conference announced that they were "glad to welcome their 'American cousin, the Reverend Moody, of Chicago,' who would now 'move a vote of thanks to the noble Earl' who had presided on this occasion."

> "With refreshing frankness and an utter disregard for conventionalities and mere compliments," as Henry Clay Trumbull was later to describe the event, "Mr. Moody burst upon the audience with the bold announcement: 'The chairman has made two mistakes. To begin with, I'm not the "Reverend" Mr. Moody at all. I'm plain Dwight L. Moody, a Sabbath school worker. And then I'm not your "American cousin"! By the grace of God, I'm your brother, who is interested with you in our Father's work for his children. And now about this vote of thanks to "the noble Earl" for being our chairman this evening. I don't see why we should thank him, any more than he should thank us. When at one time they offered to thank our Mr. Lincoln for presiding over a meeting in Illinois, he stopped it. He said he'd tried to do his duty, and they'd tried to do theirs. He thought it was an even thing all around.' That fairly took the breath away from Mr.

> Moody's hearers, [Trumbull concluded, but its] novelty was delightful, and Mr. Moody carried his English hearers from that time on."[37]

Moody hated "pretension and hypocrisy." God wants us "to be real. Let us not appear to be more than we are," rather "let us be real men and women." After all, "God hates a sham." Moody believed the frequent tendency of Christians to put on "sanctimonious" airs when we "come into the house of God" is "wrong" and unacceptable to God. "Every place ought to be holy to a true child of God."[38]

Moody's Disarming Sincerity

A second reason for Moody's broad public appeal was his disarming sincerity. John Pollock, in his delightful biography of Moody, describes the stormy visit to Cambridge University that Moody and Sankey had in November of 1882.[39] Moody had been invited by J. E. K. Studd of Trinity College, the president of the Cambridge Inter-Collegiate Christian Union, to hold a series of meetings for members of the faculty, the local community, and the nearly thirty-five hundred undergraduate students. The Corn Exchange was secured for the Sunday evening meetings and the gymnasium in Market Passage for the weekday evenings. A large choir of university men was assembled to provide some of the music, and handwritten personal invitations were sent to every member of the student body.

"There never was a place," Moody later admitted, "that I approached with greater anxiety than

Cambridge. Never having had the privilege of a university education I was nervous about meeting university men." He had good reason for concern. For as the first public service began in the cavernous Corn Exchange on Sunday evening, November 5, there sat before him some twenty-five hundred people—including seventeen hundred students in cap and gown. "Laughing and talking and rushing for seats near their friends," the students seemed interested in little save the pyramid of chairs that some students were constructing or the firecrackers with which others were enjoying an early start to Guy Fawkes Day.

In that rather raucous atmosphere, the prayers were greeted by shouts of "Hear, hear!" instead of "Amen," the hymns were followed by college songs, and Ira Sankey's first vocal solo was met "with jeers and loud demands for an encore." It was for D. L. Moody, however, that the students reserved their loudest and most vigorous jeers. Loud laughter, shouts of "Well Done!" and regular guffaws greeted the strange pronunciations and grammatical errors in Moody's preaching. Retaining his good humor to the end, however, Moody continued to press the claims of Christ. Following the meeting, the "Christian Union men returned to their colleges 'with heavy hearts.' Their opponents laughed. 'If uneducated men will come to teach the Varsity,' commented Gerald Lander, a Trinity College student and one of the leaders of the opposition, 'they deserve to be snubbed.' "[40]

While others complained and argued, Moody turned to prayer. Knowing that the situation was beyond his abilities, he collected a hundred and fifty mothers to pray for the university students they so much wanted to reach. By Wednesday evening, the atmosphere had changed. At the close of the service, Moody invited any who wished to give their lives to Christ to gather in the gymnasium fencing-room. "Not a man moved," and "Moody repeated the appeal." Not until the third or fourth appeal, in fact, did anyone move. Then "a young Trinity man, 'amidst an awful stillness,' left his place, and 'half hiding his face in his gown, bounded up the stairs two at a time.' Another followed. Soon the gymnasium reverberated with clatter, man after man. The choir sang again. Moody said, 'I never saw the gowns look so well before,' and led Sankey up the stairs. Of fifty-two men counted in the gallery, one was Gerald Lander." God's grace and the disarming sincerity of his servant had won the day.

Moody's Winsome Humility

A third reason for Moody's broad appeal was his winsome humility. Given the great success that Moody enjoyed, especially during his later years, it is really quite remarkable how free he remained from the temptations of pride and arrogance. If anyone could have boasted of his accomplishments, surely it would have been Moody. Yet he remained staunchly convinced that it was God—not he—who deserved whatever glory might come from such endeavors.

We get a beautiful glimpse of that aspect of Moody's life in the relationship he had with his children. Emma, Will, and Paul all considered their father a kind of "stout and bearded Peter Pan." The family loved being together and the house was frequently filled with laughter and fun. "The Moody children never had any doubts that theirs was the best father in the world." He wanted his children "to become strong Christians," of course, but he was also determined to keep the home as free as possible from spiritual arm-twisting or "self-conscious pious talk."

When Moody was away from home, he and the children would often exchange letters. On one such occasion, in December 1886, Will wrote to express the rebellion he felt against the religion of his parents. Moody's reply is both instructive and deeply moving.

> Yours is in hand & I am glad you told me for I would rather have you come to me with your faults than to hide them. Of course I am very sorry you were ever tempted to smoke. I was in hopes it would never be a temptation to you but the thing that hurts me worst is that you have no desire to know Christ. Sometimes my heart is so heavy & sad to think that you have such contempt for one that has done so much for your mother & father, all that we are or have has come from him & you have been saved from an early grave I think in answer to prayer & now when you have strength & health given you & are now in a position to do good you turn against the truest & best friend you will ever have. For the life of me I cannot see why you should have taken such a dislike to Christ.
>
> I sometimes think it is my fault, if I had lived more consistent you would not be so disgusted

with what is so near my heart. Last Sept. was the happiest month of my life when I thought you had really started for the kingdom of God but when I returned home & found you were more indifferent than ever my heart sank within me. I have not talked much with you for fear I would turn you more & more against him whom I love more than all the world & if I have ever said or done any thing unbecoming a Christian father I want you to forgive me & would rather die than to stand in your way.

The thing that shames me is that I am preaching to others & my son does not believe in the gospel I preach. It was hard preaching last night after reading your letter, it seemed as if I could almost hear a voice saying look to home. I have always felt when a father & mother both were Christians & their children were not that there was something decidedly wrong with them & I still think so & last night I was speaking to parents & how my life condemned me—I have tried not to make religion offensive in my home & if I thought I had neglected to do all my duty towards my three children I think I would rather die than to live. I have tried to make your home life as pleasant as I can & have done all in my power to make you happy. I thought when I started the schools it would bring a good influence into the town for my own family & day & night my desire and prayer has been that we might all be united in Spirit but you seem to hate the things I love. The gulf seems to grow darker & deeper every day between us & I am afraid in 5 years there will be nothing in common between us. If you choose the world for your portion you will die some day a sad disappointed man I am sure. Dear Willie the world will deceive

> you but never satisfy you. You have not been happy for a year & your discontent has increased & it has hurt your father & mother far more than you will ever know until you become a father yourself.
>
> I hope there is no sin that is keeping you from Christ but times I am afraid there is something that I do not know in your life but I pray God to show it to you if there is & may God help you confess it & turn against it. I have never prayed for you as I do now. I think it is a crisis in your life & now dear Willie take this in the same spirit it is written—your Father D L Moody.[41]

Although some years were to pass before his prayers were answered, Moody's letter reflects the kind of winsome humility that God used to touch not only his son but an entire world.

Moody's Contagious Enthusiasm

A fourth reason for Moody's wide appeal was his contagious enthusiasm. "I have yet to find," Moody liked to say, "that God ever uses" a person who "is all the time looking on the dark side, and is all the time talking about the obstacles" and is "discouraged and cast down." These are the Christians who "kill everything they touch. There is no life in them." Rather, Moody was convinced, we must "be of good courage," remembering that "the God [who] commands us to work in his vineyard" has "all power in heaven and earth."

"I don't think a little enthusiasm would hurt the church at the present time," Moody liked to say.

"There may be barriers in our path, but God can remove them. There may be difficulties in the way, but he can overcome them." Until believers are baptized "with the spirit of enthusiasm" and anointed "with the Holy Ghost," our ministries will languish. Many Christians today, Moody was convinced, have become "crusty and sour, and they discourage every one they meet by their fault finding. That is not what we want." Rather, we need cheerleaders and enthusiastic participants in the great work that God has left us to do. "We can have enthusiasm in business" and "we can have enthusiasm in politics," and "no one complains of that." But get "a little fire in the church" and the cry of "false enthusiasm" begins to be heard. While the Scriptures warn us against "zeal without knowledge," we should be equally concerned about "knowledge without zeal." Indeed, it won't hurt us a bit to infuse the Lord's work with a healthy dose of "enthusiasm and zeal." [42]

Moody's Clear Focus

A fifth reason for Moody's appeal was the clarity of his focus. "Many people are working and working," Moody once said, "like children on a rocking horse. It is a beautiful motion, but there is no progress."[43] Moody believed, as he often commented in his sermons, that "every man and woman" has been given a task to do by the Lord of the universe and that they should give every ounce of energy to fulfilling it for the glory of God. There are many, he was convinced, "that are willing to do great things for the Lord" but only a few who are "willing to do little things."

The work we do, of course, must be done from the right motivation. In his sermon "Pray and Work," Moody complained: "I am tired of the word duty; tired of hearing duty, duty, duty." Some people "go to church because it is their duty. They go to prayer-meeting because it is their duty." But one can never reach another's heart simply out of duty. "Suppose I told my wife I loved her because it was my duty—what would she say?" Suppose I tell my mother that I come to see her "because it is my duty." What would she think? Our "churches would soon be filled if outsiders could find that people in them loved them when they came." Indeed, "if the Savior could die for the world," Moody concluded, then why "can't we work for it?"[44]

Moody himself was relentless—often to the point of physical collapse—in his pursuit of the work he believed God had given him to do. Throughout his lifetime, he carried a load that would have crushed the average man. Yet, he retained a remarkably upbeat spirit despite enormous financial pressures and numerous setbacks. His one great passion was to introduce people to Christ, and to that one great end he willingly structured everything he did.

Moody's Generous Spirit

A sixth reason for Moody's wide appeal was his generous spirit. In an age of sometimes petty doctrinal and ecclesiastical divisions, Moody called again and again for Christian love and unity. Labeled "the grandfather of ecumenism" by John Pollock, Moody believed that the test of true Christianity is love. Indeed, "God's work cannot be done without love."[45]

Indeed, if love is not the motivation for our ministries, our "work is for naught. If a man in the church ain't sound in his faith," Moody argued, "we draw our ecclesiastical sword and cut his head right off." If, however, he is not "sound in love," we "do nothing." "The great want in our churches is the want of love in them."[46]

Moody's Heartwarming Stories

A seventh reason for Moody's popular appeal was the heartwarming stories he told. A good example, from his sermon "Good News," tells the story of an English couple with an only son. (Readers may wish to read the story in full at this point. It may be found on pages 11–13.) One day, as Moody recounted the story, the father and son had a bitter quarrel, which led to many years of estrangement. Finally, at the mother's deathbed, they were reconciled. After telling the story, Moody pleaded with his listeners, "Sinner, that is only a faint type, a poor illustration, because God is not angry with you. I bring you tonight to the dead body of Christ. I ask you to look at the wounds in his hands and feet, and the wound in his side. And I ask you, 'Will you not be reconciled?' When he left heaven, he went down into the manger that he might get hold of the vilest sinner, and put the hand of the wayward prodigal into that of the Father, and he died that you and I might be reconciled. If you take my advice," Moody then concluded, "you will not sleep tonight until you are reconciled [to God]."[47]

Moody's Continuing Legacy

These seven characteristics of Moody's life and work—his refreshing honesty, his disarming sincerity, his winsome humility, his clear focus, his contagious enthusiasm, his generous spirit, and his heartwarming stories—are not, of course, meant to exhaust the list of possible reasons for his enormous appeal to millions of listeners and readers in his day and ours. Rather, they serve merely as appetizers to prepare the reader for the sumptuous feast awaiting them just ahead, for Moody's sermons are the windows through which we can see this remarkable man most clearly.

One hundred years have passed since the *New York Times* carried the headline announcing "Dwight L. Moody Is Dead"—and just as there were in his day, there are those in ours who "don't believe a word of it," for both the man and the message are as alive today as they were a century ago—calling men and women to Christ and enlisting them in the spread of the gospel around the world.

Notes

1. William R. Moody, *The Life of Dwight L. Moody by His Son* (New York and Chicago: Revell, 1900), frontispiece.

2. *The New York Times* (December 23, 1899), 1. See also *The Boston Daily Globe* (December 23, 1899), 1.

3. See, for example, Lyle W. Dorsett, *A Passion for Souls: The Life of D. L. Moody* (Chicago: Moody, 1997); James F. Findlay, Jr., *Dwight L. Moody: American Evangelist, 1837–1899* (Chicago: University of Chicago Press, 1969); John C. Pollock, *Moody: A Biography* (1984; repr., Grand Rapids: Baker, 1997); Stanley N. Gundry, *Love Them In: The Life and Theology of D. L. Moody* (1976; repr., Grand Rapids: Baker, 1982); and William Moody, *The Life;* idem, *D. L. Moody* (New York: Macmillan, 1930).

4. Wilbur M. Smith, *An Annotated Bibliography of D. L. Moody* (Chicago: Moody, 1948), 1–96.

5. Wilbur M. Smith estimates that Moody preached approximately 260 different sermons, some of them 60 or 70 times, during the years of his public ministry. These focused on about 96 different subjects and were drawn from approximately 160 biblical texts (119 from the New Testament). See Wilbur M. Smith, ed., *The Best of D. L. Moody* (Chicago: Moody, 1971), 13–15; and *Annotated Bibliography,* 105–8.

6. *The London Discourses of Mr. D. L. Moody as Delivered in the Agricultural Hall and Her Majesty's Opera House,* published in London in 1875, was the first publication of Moody's sermons. Addresses by D. L. Moody, *The Blood, Christ All in All, Christ's Boundless Compassion, Eight "I Wills" of Christ, Heaven, Naaman the Syrian, The New Birth, The Penitent Thief, The Way of Salvation, Wondrous Love, The Prophet Daniel, The Right Kind of Faith, The Scarlet Thread,* and *Twelve Sermons* were published the same year.

7. Smith, *Best of D. L. Moody,* 13–15.

8. See "The Unconventional Dwight L. Moody," *Christian History* 25 (9, 1990): frontispiece; and Dorsett, *A Passion for Souls,* dust jacket.

9. For a fascinating description of the Moody family history see the first chapter of William R. Moody's biography of his father.

10. John C. Pollock, "D. L. Moody and Revival," in John D. Woodbridge, ed., *Great Leaders of the Christian Church* (Chicago: Moody, 1988), 340–42.

11. See Dorsett, *A Passion for Souls,* 28–33.

12. William Moody, *The Life,* 35.

13. David Maas, "The Life and Times of D. L. Moody," *Christian History* 25 (9, 1): 5–11.

14. By 1890, Boston's population had swelled to 560,892. For a helpful interpretation of these developments see Sydney E. Ahlstrom, *A Religious History of the American People* (New Haven: Yale University Press, 1972), 731–872, statistics from p. 735.

15. Cecil Woodham-Smith, *The Great Hunger: Ireland, 1845–1849* (New York: Harper & Row, 1962). See also Marcus Lee Hansen, *The Immigrant in American History* (New York: Harper Torchbooks, 1964). For a superb study of the Christian response to urbanization and industrialization see Norris Magnuson, *Salvation in the Slums* (Grand Rapids: Baker, 1990).

16. William Moody, *The Life,* 36.

17. A copy of Edward Kimball's "Reminiscences of Moody" can be found in the Yale University archives.

18. William Moody, *The Life,* 41.

19. For a helpful discussion of the date of Moody's conversion see Dorsett, *A Passion for Souls,* 48.

20. Account taken from an unpublished letter, Mervin E. Rosell to Garth M. Rosell, July 15, 1995.

21. Northfield, Mount Hermon, and Moody Bible Institute. See James Findlay, "Moody, 'Gapmen,' and the Gospel: The Early Days of Moody Bible Institute," *Church History* (September 1962): 322–35; Donald A. Wells, "D. L. Moody and His Schools: An Historical Analysis of an Educational Ministry" (Ph.D. diss., Boston University, 1972); and Bernard R. DeRemer, *Moody Bible Institute: A Pictorial History* (Chicago: Moody, 1960).

22. Allan Fisher, "D. L. Moody's Contribution to Christian Publishing," *Christian History* 25 (9, 1990): 32–33.

23. For an excellent study of Moody and Sankey's 1876 Chicago revival see Darrel M. Robertson, *The Chicago Revival, 1876: Society and Revivalism in a Nineteenth-Century City* (Metuchen, N.J.: Scarecrow Press, 1989).

24. Smith, *Annotated Bibliography,* 73.

25. Stanley N. Gundry, "Grand Themes of D. L. Moody," *Christianity Today* (December 20, 1974): 4–5.

26. President U. S. Grant is known to have attend his revivals, and President Abraham Lincoln visited his mission school.

27. Dorsett, *A Passion for Souls,* 124.

28. See Mark Fackler's discussion, "The World Has Yet to See, . . ." *Christian History* 25 (9, 1990): 10.

29. Dorsett, *A Passion for Souls,* 59–61.

30. William Moody, *The Life,* 56.

31. Kathryn Teresa Long, *The Revival of 1857–58: Interpreting an American Religious Awakening* (New York: Oxford University Press, 1998). Compare Garth M. Rosell and Richard A. G. Dupuis, eds., *The Memoirs of Charles G. Finney* (Grand Rapids: Zondervan, 1997), 559–614.

32. William Moody, *The Life,* 62–72.

33. These remarkable meetings are described in detail in William Moody, *The Life,* 152–253.

34. Pollock, "D. L. Moody and Revival," in Woodbridge, *Great Leaders of the Christian Church,* 341. For interesting parallels in the later ministry of Billy Graham see Garth M. Rosell, "Grace under Fire," *Christianity Today* (November 13, 1995): 30–34.

35. David W. Bebbington, "How Moody Changed Revivalism," *Christian History* 25 (9, 1): 22–25. Compare Donald W. Dayton, *Discovering an Evangelical Heritage* (1976; repr., Peabody, Mass.: Hendrickson, 1988), passim; and Garth M. Rosell, "Charles G. Finney: His Place in the Stream of American Evangelicalism," in Leonard I. Sweet, ed., *The Evangelical Tradition in America* (Macon, Ga.: Mercer University Press, 1997), 131–47; idem, "A Speckled

Bird: Charles G. Finney's Contribution to Higher Education," *Fides et Historia* (Summer, 1993): 55–74.

36. See Gundry, "Grand Themes of D. L. Moody," 4–6; and "The Three Rs of Moody's Theology," *Christian History* 25 (9,1990): 16–19.

37. Account provided in William Moody, *D. L. Moody,* 132.

38. Gundry, "Grand Themes of D. L. Moody," 5.

39. For the full account and quotations see William Moody, *The Life,* 349–59; and Pollock, *Moody,* 199–209.

40. William Moody, *The Life,* 351.

41. D. L. Moody to W. R. Moody, December 8, 1886, Moody Papers, Powell Collection, East Northfield, Massachusetts.

42. Quotations taken from the sermon, "Courage and Work," *Glad Tidings* (New York: E. B. Treat, 1877), 32–42, and included in this collection.

43. Gundry, "Grand Themes of D. L. Moody," 5.

44. Moody's understandings of work and vocation seem to have been shaped by the great Puritan tradition in which his own family had been nourished: namely, the double call of God to all Christians—first to salvation and then to that vocation (or those vocations) that will bring glory to God and serve the common good. See Leland Ryken, *Work and Leisure in Christian Perspective* (Portland, Ore.: Multnomah, 1987); W. R. Forrester, *Christian Vocation* (New York: Charles Scribner's Sons, 1953); and Garth M. Rosell, "Call to Ministry: Some Historical Reflections" (unpublished paper, Ockenga Institute, Gordon-Conwell Theological Seminary, South Hamilton, Mass., 1997).

45. John C. Pollock, "Dwight L. Moody—Grandfather of Ecumenism?" *Christianity Today* (November 23, 1962): 29–30.

46. Quotations from Gundry, "Grand Themes of D. L. Moody," 4–6.

47. D. L. Moody, "Good News," in *Twelve Select Sermons* (Chicago: Revell, 1880), 32–44.

Good News 1

1 CORINTHIANS 15:1

Moreover, brethren, I declare unto you the gospel which I preached unto you, which also ye have received, and wherein ye stand.

I do not think there is a word in the English language so little understood as the word *gospel*. We hear it every day, and we have heard it from our earliest childhood, yet there are many people, and even many Christians, who do not really know what it means. I believe I was a child of God a long time before I really knew. The word *gospel* means "God's spell," or good spell, or in other words, "good news."

The gospel is good tidings of great joy. No better news ever came out of heaven than the gospel. No better news ever fell upon the ears of the family of man than the gospel. When the angels came down to proclaim the tidings, what did they say to those shepherds on the plains of Bethlehem? "Behold I bring you *sad* tidings?" No! "Behold, I bring you *bad* news?" No! "Behold, I bring you *good* tidings of *great joy*, which shall be to all people; for unto you is born this day, in the city of David, a Savior."

If those shepherds had been like a good many people at the present time, they would have said, "We do not believe it is good news. It is all excitement. These angels want to get up a revival. These angels are trying to excite us. Don't you believe them." That is what Satan is saying now. "Don't you believe the gospel is good news; it will only make you miserable." He knows the moment a man believes good news, he just receives it. And no one who is under the power of the devil really believes that the gospel is good news. But these shepherds believed the message that the angels brought, and their hearts were filled with joy.

If a boy came with a dispatch to someone here, could you not tell by the receiver's looks what kind of a message it was? If it brought good news you would see it in his face in a moment. If it told him that his boy, away in some foreign land, a prodigal son, had come to himself, like the one in the fifteenth chapter of Luke, do you not think that father's face would light up with joy? And if his wife were here, he would not wait till they got home, or till she asked for it, he would pass it over to her, and her face would brighten too, as she shared his joy. But the tidings that the gospel brings are more glorious than that. We are dead in trespasses and sins, and the gospel offers life. We are enemies to God, and the gospel offers reconciliation. The world is in darkness, and the gospel offers light. Because man will not believe the gospel that Christ is the light of the world, the world is dark today. But the moment a man believes, the light from Calvary crosses his path and he walks in an unclouded sun.

I want to tell you why I like the gospel. It is because it has been the very best news I have ever heard. That is just why I like to preach it, because it has done me so much good. No man can ever tell what it has done for him, but I think I can tell what it has *undone*. It has taken out of my path three of the bitterest enemies I ever had.

Death

There is that terrible enemy mentioned in 1 Corinthians 15, the last enemy, *death*. The gospel has taken it out of the way. My mind very often rolls back some twenty years now, before I was converted, and I think how dark it used to seem, as I thought of the future. I well remember how I used to look on death as a terrible monster, how he used to throw his dark shadow across my path; how I trembled as I thought of the terrible hour when he should come for me; how I thought I should like to die of some lingering disease, such as consumption, so that I might know when he was coming. It was the custom in our village to toll from the old church bell the age of anyone who died. Death never entered that village and tore away one of the inhabitants, but I counted the tolling of the bell. Some times it was seventy, sometimes eighty; sometimes it would be away down among the teens; sometimes it would toll out the death of someone of my own age. It made a solemn impression upon me. I felt a coward then. I thought of the cold hand of death feeling for the cords of life. I thought of being launched forth to spend my eternity in an unknown land.

As I looked into the grave, and saw the sexton throw the earth on the coffin lid, "Earth to earth; ashes to ashes; dust to dust," it seemed like the death knell to my soul. But that is all changed now. The grave has lost its terror. As I go on towards heaven I can shout, "O death! where is thy sting?" and I hear the answer rolling down from Calvary—"buried in the bosom of the Son of God." He took the sting right out of death for me, and received it into his own bosom. Take a hornet and pluck the sting out; you are not afraid of it after that any more than of a fly. So death has lost its sting. That last enemy has been overcome, and I can look on death as a crushed victim.

All that death can get now is this old Adam, and I do not care how quickly I get rid of it. I shall get a glorified body, a resurrection body, a body much better than this. Suppose death should come stealing up into this pulpit, and lay his icy hand upon my heart, and it should cease to throb, I should rise to the better world to be present with the King. The gospel has made an enemy a friend. What a glorious thought, that when you die you but sink into the arms of Jesus, to be borne to the land of everlasting rest! "To die," the apostle says, "is gain." I can imagine when they laid our Lord in Joseph's tomb one might have seen death sitting over that sepulchre, saying, "I have him, he is my victim. He said he was the resurrection and the life. Now I hold him in my cold embrace. They thought he was never going to die; but see him now. He has had to pay tribute to me." Never! The glorious morning comes, the Son of man bursts asunder the bands of death, and rises, a Conqueror, from the grave. "Because I live," he shouts, "ye shall live also." Yes, *ye shall live also*—is it not good news? Ah, my friends, there is no bad news about a gospel which makes it so sweet to live, so sweet to die.

Sin

Another terrible enemy that troubled me was *sin*. What a terrible hour I thought it would be, when my sins from childhood, every secret thought, every evil desire, everything done in the dark, should be brought to the light, and spread out before an assembled universe! Thank God, these thoughts are gone. The gospel tells me my sins are all put away in Christ. Out of love to me he has taken all my sins and cast them behind his back. That is a safe place for them. God never turns back; he always marches on. He will never see your sins if they are behind his back—that is one of his own illustrations. Satan has to get behind God to find them. How far away are they, and can they ever come back again? *"As far as the east is from the west, so far hath He removed our transgressions from us.*" Not some of them; he takes them all away. You may pile up your sins till they rise like a dark mountain, and then multiply them by ten thousand for those you cannot think of; and after you have tried to enumerate all the sins you have ever committed, just let me bring one verse in, and that mountain will melt away: "The blood of Jesus Christ, his Son, cleanseth us from all sin."

In Ireland, some time ago, a teacher asked a little boy if there was anything God could not do; and the little fellow said, "Yes; he cannot see my sins through the blood of Christ." That is just what he cannot do. The blood covers them. Is it not good news that you can get rid of sin? You come to Christ a sinner, and if you receive his gospel your sins are taken away. You are invited to do this; nay, he entreats you to do it. You are invited to make an exchange; to get rid of all your sins, and to take Christ and his righteousness in the place of them. Is not that good news?

Judgment

There is another enemy which used to trouble me a good deal—*judgment*. I used to look forward to the terrible day when I should be summoned before God. I could not tell whether I should hear the voice of Christ saying, "Depart from me, ye cursed," or whether it would be, "Enter thou into the joy of thy Lord." And I thought that till he stood before the great white throne no man could tell whether he was to be on the right hand or the left. But the gospel tells me that is already settled: "There is now no condemnation to them which are in Christ Jesus." "Verily, verily"—and when you see that word in Scripture, you may know there is something very important coming—"Verily, verily, I say unto you, he that heareth my word, and believeth on him that sent me, *hath* everlasting life, and *shall not* come into condemnation, but *is passed* from death unto life."

Well, now, *I* am not coming into judgment for sin. It is no open question. God's word has settled it. Christ was judged for me, and died in my stead, and I go free. He that believeth *hath*—h-a-t-h, hath. Is not that good news? A man prayed for me the other day that I might obtain eternal life *at last*. I could not have said "Amen" to that, if he meant it in the sense that I obtained eternal life nineteen years ago, when I was converted. What is the gift of God, if it is not eternal life? And what makes the gospel such good news? Is it not that it offers eternal life to every poor sinner who will take it? If an angel came straight from the throne of God, and proclaimed that God had sent him here to offer us any one thing we might ask—that each one should have his own petition granted—what would be your cry? There would be but one response, and the cry would make heaven ring: "Eternal life! Eternal life!" Everything else would float away into nothingness. It is life we want, life we value most. Let a man worth a million dollars be on a wrecked vessel, and if he could just save his life for six months by giving that million, he would give it in an instant. But the gospel is not a six months' gift.

The Cross of Christ

My friends, there is one spot on earth where the fear of death, of sin, and of judgment need never trouble us, the only safe spot on earth where the sinner can stand—Calvary. Out in our western country, in the autumn, when men go hunting, and there has not been any rain for months, sometimes the prairie grass catches fire. Sometimes, when the wind is strong, the flames may be seen rolling along, twenty feet high, destroying man and beast in their onward rush. When the frontiersmen see what is coming, what do they do to escape? They know they cannot run as fast as the fire can run. Not the fleetest horse can escape it. They just take a match and light the grass around them. The flames sweep onwards; they take their stand in the burnt district, and are safe. They hear the flames roar as they come along; they see death bearing down upon them with resistless fury, but they do not fear. They do not even tremble as the ocean of flame surges around them, for over the place where they stand the fire has already passed, and there is no danger. There is nothing for the fire to burn. And there is one spot on earth that God has swept over. Eighteen hundred years ago the storm burst on Calvary, and the Son of God took it into his own bosom, and now, if we take our stand by the Cross, we are safe for time and for eternity.

Sinner, would you be safe tonight? Would you be free from the condemnation of the sins that are past, from the power of the temptations that are to come? Then take your stand on the Rock of Ages. Let death, let the grave, let the judgment come, the victory is Christ's and yours through him. Oh, will you not receive this gospel tonight—this wonderful message?

True Freedom in Christ

Some people, when the gospel is preached, put on a long face, as if they had to attend a funeral, or witness an execution or hear some dry lecture or sermon. It was my privilege to go into Richmond with General Grant's army. I had not been long there before it was announced that the Negroes were going to have a jubilee meeting. These people were just coming into liberty; their chains were falling off, and they were just awakening to the fact that they were free. I thought it would be a great event, and I went down to the African Church, one of the largest in the South, and found it crowded. One of the Negro chaplains of a northern regiment had offered to speak. I have heard many eloquent men in Europe and in America, but I do not think I ever heard eloquence such as I heard that day. He said, "Mothers! You rejoice today; you are for ever free! That little child has been torn from your embrace, and sold off to some distant state for the last time. Your hearts are never to be broken again in that way; you are free." The women clapped their hands and shouted at the top of their voices. "Glory, glory to God." It was good news to them, and they believed it. It filled them full of joy. Then he turned to the young men, and said, "Young men! You rejoice today; you have heard the crack of the slave-driver's whip for the last time; your posterity shall be free; young men rejoice today, you are for ever free!" And they clapped their hands, and shouted, "Glory to God!" They believed the good tidings. "Young maidens!" He said, "you rejoice today. You have been put on the auction block and sold for the last time; you are free—forever free!" They believed it, and lifting up their voices, shouted, "Glory be to God!" I never was in such a meeting. They *believed* that it was good news to them.

My friends, I bring you even better tidings than that. No man or woman ever had such a mean, wicked, cruel master as those that are serving Satan. Do I speak to a man who is a slave to strong drink? Christ can give you strength to hurl the cup from you, and make you a sober man, a loving husband, a kind father. Yes, poor wife of the drunkard, he gives you good news; your husband may become a sober man again. And you, poor sinner, you who have been so rebellious and wayward, the gospel brings a message of forgiveness to you. God wants you to be reconciled to him. "Be ye reconciled unto God." It is his message to you—a message of friendship.

A Story of Reconciliation

There was an Englishman who had an only son; and only sons are sometimes spoiled and ruined. This boy became very headstrong, and very often he and his father had trouble. One day they had a quarrel, and the father was very angry, and so was the son; and the father said he wished the boy would leave home and never come back. The boy said he would go, and would not come into his father's house again till he sent for him. The father said he would never send for him. Well, away went the boy. But though the father gave up on the boy, the mother did not, for there is no love on earth so strong as a mother's love. A great many things may separate a man and his wife; a great many things may separate a father from a son; but there is nothing in the wide world that can ever separate a true mother from her child.

Well, the mother began to write, and plead with the boy to write to his father first, and he would forgive him; but the boy said, "I will never go home till father asks me." Then she plead with the father, but the father said, "No, I will never ask him." At last the mother came down to her sick-bed, brokenhearted, and when she was given up by the physicians to die, the husband, anxious to gratify her last wish, wanted to know if there was nothing he could do for her before she died. The mother gave him a look; he well knew what it meant. Then she said, "Yes, there is one thing you can do. You can send for my boy. That is the only wish on earth you can gratify. If you do not pity him and love him when I am dead and gone, who will?" "Well," said the father, "I will send word to him that you want to see him." "No," she said, "you know he will not come for me. If ever I see him you must send for him." At last the father went to his office and wrote a dispatch in his own name, asking the boy to come home. As soon as he got the invitation from his father he started off to see his dying mother. When he opened the door to go in he found his mother dying, and his father by the bedside. The father heard the door open, and saw the boy, but instead of going to meet him he went to another part of the room, and refused to speak to him. His mother seized his hand—how she had longed to press it! She kissed him, and then said, "Now, my son, just speak to your father. You speak first, and it will all be over." But the boy said, "No mother, I will not speak to him until he speaks to me."

She took her husband's hand in one hand and the boy's in the other, and spent her dying moments in trying to bring about a reconciliation. Then just as she was expiring—she could not speak—so she put the hand of the wayward boy into the hand of the father, and passed away! The boy looked at the mother, and the father at the wife, and at last the father's heart broke, and he opened his arms, and took that boy to his bosom, and by that body they were reconciled. Sinner, that is only a faint type, a poor illustration, because God is not angry with you. I bring you tonight to the dead body of Christ.

I ask you to look at the wounds in his hands and feet, and the wound in his side. And I ask you, "Will you not be reconciled?" When he left heaven, he went down into the manger that he might get hold of the vilest sinner, and put the hand of the wayward prodigal into that of the Father, and he died that you and I might be reconciled. If you take my advice you will not sleep tonight until you are reconciled. "Be ye reconciled to God." Oh, this gospel of reconciliation! My friends, is it not a glad gospel?

Good News

You need not ask, "For whom is this good news?" It is for yourself. If you would like Christ's own word for it, come with me to that scene in Jerusalem where the disciples are bidding him farewell. Calvary with all its horrors is behind him; Gethsemane is over, and Pilate's judgment hall is in the past. He has passed the grave, and is about to take his place at the right hand of the Father. Around him stands his little band of disciples, the little church he was to leave behind him to be his witnesses. The hour of parting has come, and he has some "last words" for them. Is he thinking about himself in these closing moments? Is he thinking about the throne that is waiting him, and the Father's smile that will welcome him to heaven? Is he going over in memory the scenes of the past; or is he thinking of the friends who have followed him so far, who will miss him so much when he is gone? No, he is thinking about *you*.

You imagined he would think of those who loved him? No, sinner, he thought of you then. He thought of his enemies, those who shunned him, those who despised him, those who killed him. He thought of those who would hate him, of those who would have none of his gospel, of those who would say it was too good to be true, of those who would make excuse that he never died for *them*. And then turning to his disciples, his heart bursting with compassion, he gave his farewell charge: "Go ye into *all* the world and preach the gospel *to every creature*."

I can imagine Peter saying, "Lord, do you really mean that we shall preach the gospel to *every* creature?" "Yes, Peter." "Shall we go back to Jerusalem and preach the gospel to those Jerusalem sinners who murdered you?" "Yes, Peter, go back and tarry there until you are endued with power from on high. Offer the gospel to them first. Go search out that man who spat in my face; tell him I forgive him; there is nothing in my heart but love for him. Go, search out the man who put that cruel crown of thorns on my brow; tell him I will have a crown ready for him in my kingdom, if he will accept salvation; there shall not be a thorn in it, and he shall wear it for ever and ever in the kingdom of his Redeemer. Find out that man who took the reed from my hand, and smote my head, driving the thorns deeper into my brow. If he will accept salvation as a gift, I will give him a scepter, and with it he shall hold sway over the nations of the earth. Yes, I will allow him to sit with me upon my throne. Go, seek that man who struck me with the palm of his hand; find him and preach the gospel to him; tell him that the blood of Jesus Christ cleanseth from all sin, and my blood was shed for him freely." Yes, I can imagine him saying, "Go, seek out that poor soldier who drove the spear into my side; tell him that there is a nearer way to my heart than that. Tell him that I forgive him freely; and tell him I will make him a soldier of the cross, and my banner over him shall be love."

The Gospel Is for Everyone

I thank God that the gospel is to be preached to *every* creature. I thank God the commission is so free. There is no one so far gone, but the grace of God can reach him; no one so desperate but that he can forgive him. Yes, I thank God I can preach the gospel to the man or the woman who is as dark as hell itself. I thank God for the "whosoevers" of the invitations of Christ. "God so loved the world that he gave his only begotten Son, that *whosoever* believeth on him should not perish, but have everlasting life," and "*Whosoever will,* let him take the water of life freely."

I heard of a woman once who thought there was no promise in the Bible for her, they were all for other people. One day she got a letter, and when she opened it, found it was not for her at all, but for some other woman of the same name. It led her to ask herself, "If I should find some promise in the Bible directed to *me,* how should I know that it meant *me,* and not some other woman?" But she found out that she must simply take God at his word, and include herself among the "whosoevers" and the "every creatures" to whom the gospel is freely preached. I know that word "whosoever" means every man, every woman, every child in this wide world. It means that boy down there, that gray-haired man, that maiden in the blush of youth, that young man breaking a mother's heart, that drunkard steeped in misery and sin. O my friends, will you not believe this good news? Will you not receive this wonderful gospel of Christ? Will you not believe, poor sinner, that it means *you?* Will you say it is too good to be true?

The State Prison

I was in Ohio a few years ago, and was invited to preach in the state prison. Eleven hundred convicts were brought into the chapel, and all sat in front of me. After I had got through the preaching, the chaplain said to me: "Mr. Moody, I want to tell you of a scene which occurred in this room. A few years ago, our commissioners went to the governor of the state, and got him to promise that he would pardon five men for good behavior. The governor consented, with this understanding—that the record was to be kept secret, and that at the end of six months the five men highest on the roll should receive a pardon, regardless of who or what they were. At the end of six months the prisoners were all brought into the chapel; the commissioners came up, and the president stood up on the platform, and putting his hand in his pocket, brought out some papers, and said, 'I hold in my hand pardons for five men.'" The chaplain told me he never witnessed anything on earth like it. Every man was as still as death; many were deadly pale, and the suspense was awful; it seemed as if every heart had ceased to beat. The commissioner went on to tell them how they had got the pardon; but the chaplain interrupted him. "Before you make your speech, read out the names. This suspense is awful." So he read out the first name, "Reuben Johnson will come and get his pardon"; and he held it out, but none came forward. He said to the governor, "Are all the prisoners here?" The governor told him they were all there. Then he said again, "Reuben Johnson will come and get his pardon. It is signed and sealed by the governor. He is a free man." Not one moved. The chaplain told me he looked right down where Reuben was; he was well known; he had been nineteen years at the prison, and many were looking round to see him spring to his feet. But he himself was looking round to see the fortunate man who had got his pardon. Finally the chaplain caught his eye and said, "Reuben, you are the man." Reuben turned round and looked behind him to see where Reuben was. The chaplain said the second time, "Reuben, *you* are the man"; and the second time he looked round, thinking it must be some other Reuben.

So often we do not believe the gospel is for us. We think it is too good, and pass it over our shoulders to the next person. But *you* are the person tonight.

The chaplain could see where Reuben was, and he had to say three times, “Reuben, come and get your pardon.” At last the truth began to steal over the old man; he got up and came along down the hall, trembling from head to foot, and when he got the pardon he looked at it, and went back to his seat, and buried his face in his hands, and wept. When the prisoners got into the ranks to go back to the cells, Reuben got into the ranks too, and the chaplain had to call to him, “Reuben, get out of the ranks; you are a free man, you are no longer a prisoner.” And Reuben stepped out of the ranks. He was free!

Reuben’s pardon was for good character and good behavior. But God gives out pardons for those of us who have not got any character, who have been very, very bad. He offers a pardon to every sinner on earth if he will take it. I do not care who he is or what he is like. He may be the greatest libertine that ever walked the streets, or the greatest drunkard who ever lived, or a thief, or a vagabond; but I come tonight with glad tidings—the glorious gospel is for *every creature,* it is for *you*.

Come

2

ISAIAH 55:3

Incline your ear, and come unto me: hear, and your soul shall live; and I will make an everlasting covenant with you, even the sure mercies of David.

We have for our subject this afternoon the precious little word "come." I want to call your attention first to the "come" in the fifty-fifth chapter of the prophecies of Isaiah. "Incline your ear, and come unto me. Hear, and your souls shall live; and I will make an everlasting covenant with you, even the sure mercies of David."

"Incline your ear and come unto me; hear and your soul shall live." Now, I find if we get people to listen—to pause and hear the voice of God—it isn't long before they are willing to follow that voice; but it is difficult to get people to stop and listen.

The din of the world makes such a noise that the people don't hear the voice—that still, small voice. He says, "Incline your ear and come unto me." Now, if we could only get all the friends in this audience to incline their ears this afternoon—

not only your natural ears but the ears of your soul, you could be saved today. But Satan does not want you to do this; he does all he can to keep your ears from hearing. He makes you think about yourself, about your sons and daughters, your homes; but, my friends, let us forget all those things today—let us forget all our surroundings, and close our eyes to the world, and just try and listen to the word of God, and come and hear what he has to say. "Incline your ear and come unto me; hear and your soul shall live."

Turn with me, if you would, to the tenth chapter of Romans, where we read, "Faith cometh by hearing, and hearing by the word of God." These are not my words I want you to listen to—it is not my words I want you to hear this afternoon—but I want you to hear the words of this loving King who calls you to himself. What does he say? In another place we read: "Behold, I stand at the door and knock; if any man hear my voice and open the door, I will come in to him and sup with him and he with me," or "if any woman," or anyone—that's what it means, my friends—"hear my voice and open the door, I will come in to her, and will sup with her and she with me."

The Little Child

I heard of a little child some time ago who was burned. The mother had gone out and left her three children at home. The eldest left the room, and the remaining two began to play with the fire, and set the place in a blaze. When the youngest of the two saw what she had done she went into a little cupboard and fastened herself in. The remaining child went to the door and knocked and knocked, crying to her to open the door and let her take her out of the burning building, but she was too frightened to do it.

It seems to me as if this was the way with hundreds and thousands in this city. Christ stands and knocks, but we've got our hearts barred and bolted, because we don't know that he has come only to bless us. May God help you to hear, and if you listen to him and bring your burdens to him, he will bless you. He is able to open the ears of everyone here if you let him in. I was at the hotel the other night, and I had the door locked and bolted, and someone came and rapped. I shouted "Come in!" The man tried to come in, but he couldn't; I had to get up and unlock the door before he could enter. That's the way with many people today. They've got the door bolted and barred; but if you only open it to him, he will come in.

"If any man hear my voice and open the door I will come in and sup with him and he with me." Now, my friends, can you hear it? Can you hear God's voice speaking through his own word? "Incline your ear and come unto me." Just listen. You know sometimes, when you hear a man speaking whose voice you don't hear very well, and you want to hear every word the man says, you put your hand up to your ear to catch the sound clearer.

Now, listen. God says, "Incline your ear and come unto me; hear and your souls shall live; and I will make an everlasting covenant with you." Now, is it not true? Can't you hear that loving voice speaking to you, and won't you obey that voice and let him save you? But I can imagine some of you saying, "I can't hear anything." Take your ears to him and he will make you hear.

Come and See

While John and his disciples were standing, Jesus came along, and John said: "Behold the Lamb of God!" and Jesus said: "What seek ye?" "Where dwellest thou?" he asked; to which Christ replied: "Come and see"; and they obeyed him and never left him. My friends, if I could introduce you to Christ—could just get you to catch one glimpse of him; if you could but see the King in all his beauty; if you could but see him in all his loveliness, you would never forsake him, for he "shall grow up before him as a tender plant and as a root out of a dry ground; he hath no form nor comeliness, and when we shall see him there is no beauty that we should desire him." Follow him as your Savior. In order to appreciate him you have to be brought to him, but if sin has come between you and him, I cannot tell you anything about him. It is just like telling a blind man about the beauties of nature, the loveliness of the flowers, or of the world. That is the way, if sin stands between you and him, and when Christians try to tell you about the beauties of Christianity they fail, but if you come and have an interview with him you will see that you cannot help but love him; you will see that you cannot but forsake all and follow him.

I remember once hearing of a child who was born blind. He grew up to be almost a man, when a skillful physician thought he could give the man his sight. He was put under the doctor's treatment, and for a long time he worked, till at last he succeeded. But he wouldn't let the man see the light of the sun all at once, lest it would strike him blind. It had to be done gradually. So he put a lot of bandages upon his eyes and removed one after another until the last one was reached, and when it was taken off the young man began to see. When he saw the beauties of the world he upbraided his friends for not telling him of the beauties of nature. "Why, we tried to tell you about the beauties of the world, but we could not," they said. And so it is with us. All that we can do is to tell you to come and see—come and see the loveliness of Christ.

I can imagine some of you saying: "I am blind, I cannot see any beauty in him." Bring your blindness to him as you bring your deafness and he will give you sight, as he did with the blind Bartimaeus—as he did with all the blind men on earth. There was never a blind man who came to him requesting his sight whose request was not granted, and there is not a blind soul in this assembly but will be healed if you come to him. He says that's what he came for, to give sight to the blind. If you cannot see any beauty in him pray to God to give you sight.

Come and Reason

The next "come" is in the prophecies of Isaiah. "Come, now, and let us reason together," saith the Lord. "Though your sins be as scarlet, they shall be as white as snow; though they be red like crimson, they shall be as wool." I find a great many people who say their reason stands between them and God. Now, let me say here, the religion of Jesus is a matter of revelation, not of investigation. No one ever found out Christ by reason. It is a matter of revelation. Now see what he says, "Come now"—that means this afternoon—"though your sins be as scarlet, they shall be white as snow." Now he puts a pardon in the sinner's face. "Your sins may be as scarlet, they shall be white as snow."

Take the scarlet in that lady's shawl. It is a fast color. You cannot wash it out and make it white; if you tried you would only destroy the shawl. But he will make your sins white as snow, though they be as scarlet, if you come to him. Just come to him as you are, and instead of reasoning ask him to take them away. Then he will reason it out with you. The natural man does not understand spiritual things, but when a man is born of the Spirit, then it is that the spiritual things are brought out to him. A great many people want to investigate—want to reason out the Bible from back to back—but he wants us first to take a pardon. That's God's method of reasoning. He puts a pardon in the face of the sinner. "Come now." Do you think there is not reason in this? Suppose the whole plan of salvation was reasoned out to you; why, death might step in before the end of the reasoning was reached. So God puts a pardon first. If you will be influenced today you will just bring your reason to him, and ask him to give you wisdom to see divine things, and he will do it. "If any of you lacks wisdom, let him ask of God that giveth to all men liberally and upbraideth not, and it shall be given liberally."

The Infidel

A number of years ago as I was coming out of a daily prayer meeting in one of our western cities, a lady came up to me and said, "I want to have you see my husband and ask him to come to Christ." She said, "I want to have you go and see him." She told me his name, and it was of a man I had heard of before. "Why," said I, "I can't go and see your husband. He is an infidel—and I can't argue with him. He is a good deal older than I am, and it would be out of place. Then I am not much for infidel argument." "Well, Mr. Moody," she said, "that isn't what he wants. He's got enough of that. Just ask him to come to the Savior." She urged me so hard and so strong, that I consented to go. I went to the office where the judge was doing business, and told him what I had come for. He laughed at me. "You are very foolish," he said, and began to argue with me. I said, "I don't think it will be profitable for me to hold an argument with you. I have just one favor I want to ask of you, and that is, that when you are converted you will let me know." "Yes," said he with a good deal of sarcasm, "I will do that. When I am converted, I will let you know."

A year and a half after I was in that city, a servant came to the door and said, "There is a man in the front parlor who wishes to see you." When I entered the parlor, I found the judge there. He said, "I promised I would let you know when I was converted. I've been converted." "Well," said I, "I'm glad to hear it! Tell me all about it." He said his wife had gone out to a meeting one night and he was home alone, and while he was sitting there by the fire he thought: "Supposing my wife is right, and my children are right; suppose there is a heaven and hell, and I shall be separated from them." His first thought was: "I don't believe a word of it." The second thought came, "You believe in the God that created you, and that the God that created you is able to teach you. You believe that God can give you life." "Yes, the God that created me can give me life. I was too proud to get down on my knees by the fire, and I said, 'O God, teach me.' And as I prayed, I don't understand it, but it began to get very dark, and my heart got very heavy. I was afraid to tell my wife when she came to bed and I pretended to be asleep. She kneeled down beside that bed and I knew she was praying for me. I kept crying, 'O God, save me; O God, take away this burden,' but it grew darker, and the load grew heavier and heavier. All the way to my office I kept crying, 'O God, take away this load of guilt.' I gave my clerks a holiday, and just closed my office and locked the door. I fell down on my face; I cried in agony to the Lord, 'O Lord, for Christ's sake, take away this guilt.' I don't know how long it was, but it began to grow very light. I said, I wonder if this isn't what they call conversion. I think I will go and ask the minister if I am not converted. I met my wife at the door and said: 'My dear, I've been converted.' She looked in amazement. 'Oh it's a fact, I've been converted!' We went into that drawing-room and knelt down by the sofa and prayed to God to bless us." The old judge said to me, the tears trickling down his cheeks, "Mr. Moody, I've enjoyed life more in the last three months than in all the years of my life put together."

Come and Rest

The next "come" I want to call your attention to is a very sweet one: Christ says, "Come and rest." What this world wants is rest. Every man, every woman is in pursuit of rest, and yet how few have found it. How many are bearing burdens—how many have come into this hall today with great burdens on their hearts? What does Christ say? "Come unto me, all ye that labor and are heavy laden, and I will give you rest." Now a great many people have an idea that they can get rid of their burdens themselves, but they must come to him if they want to be relieved. That's what Christ came for. Come to him, for "he hath borne our griefs and carried our sorrows." There could not be a sweeter "come" than this. How many mothers are bearing burdens for their children? How many are weighed down by sin or need or an unfaithful husband? The future may look dark to you; but hear the loving voice of the Savior: "Come unto me, all ye that labor and are heavy laden, and I will give you rest." There is not a soul here in this vast audience—I don't care what the burden may be—but can lay their burden on the Lord Jesus Christ, and he will bear it for you. We can be released; we have found a resting place, and that is in the loving bosom of the Lord Jesus Christ. There is a hymn written by Dr. Horatius Bonar which expresses this much better than I can. Let me read it:

> I heard the voice of Jesus say,
> "Come unto me and rest;
> Lay down, thou weary one, lay down
> Thy head upon my breast."
>
> I came to Jesus as I was,
> Weary and worn and sad;
> I found in Him a resting place,
> And He has made me glad.
>
> I heard the voice of Jesus say,
> "Behold I freely give
> The living water—thirsty one,
> Stoop down, and drink, and live."

I came to Jesus and I drank
Of that life-giving stream;
My thirst was quenched, my soul revived,
And now I live in Him.

I heard the voice of Jesus say:
"I am this dark world's light;
Look unto me, thy morn shall rise,
And all thy day be bright."

I looked to Jesus and I found
In Him my star, my sun;
And in that light of life I'll walk,
Till trav'ling days are done.

O my friends, if you want rest today, come to him. He stands with his arms outstretched and says: "Come to me and rest." Does the world satisfy you? Are not the griefs of this world crushing many a heart here? Hear the voice of Jesus: "Come and rest." The world cannot take it from you; the world's crosses and trials will not tear it from you; he will give you peace and comfort and rest if you but come.

Come Eat and Drink

The next "come" is "Come and drink and eat." You don't have to pay anything. Salvation is like a river, flowing at the feet of everyone; and all you have to do is to stoop down and drink of this living water and never die. The world cannot give you comfort, cannot give you water to satisfy your thirst—

and every man and woman in this world is thirsty. That's the way our places of amusement are filled. People are constantly thirsting for something. But how are they filled with those amusements? They are as thirsty as ever. But if they drink the waters that he offers they will have a fountain in them springing up into everlasting life.

I remember coming down a river with some wounded soldiers. The water was very muddy, and as we had no filters they had to drink the dirty water, which did not satisfy their thirst. I remember a soldier saying, "O that I had a draught of water from my father's well." If you drink of the living water your soul will never thirst again.

Not only does he say, "Come and drink of that living water," but he says, "Come and eat." In the fifty-fifth chapter of Isaiah you are invited to come and eat. You know all that the children of Israel had to do in the wilderness was to pick up the manna and eat. They didn't have to make it. And people had just to stoop down and pick up the manna and eat, and drink from the flinty rock when the water flowed. And today the provision is brought to the door of your hearts. You haven't to go down to the earth for it, or to go up to the skies for it. It is here, and all you've got to do is to eat.

You know almost the last words of Christ after his resurrection, when, having a little fish, he said to his disciples: "Come and dine." Oh, what a sweet invitation—the invitation of the Master to his disciples, "Come and dine." I invite you now to come and dine with him; he will quench that thirst;

he will satisfy your hunger, and all you've got to do is to take him at his word.

Is there a poor thirsty one here today? I bid you come and drink of the fountain of living water; I bid you come and eat of the heavenly bread; yes, the bread made in heaven, the bread that angels feed on—for Christ himself is the bread of life.

Now, many people make a great mistake about accepting Christ. They think they've got something to do; think they've got to do some work, or that they've got to pray and wrestle before taking him; they think it is a question of performances whether they are saved or not. Now, it is a question of simply taking what God offers you. I remember when I was out on the Pacific coast, a man took me through his house, out on his lands, and showed me his orchards, and then said: "Mr. Moody, you are a guest of mine, and I want you to feel perfectly at home; do what you like." Well, after this man said this, you don't suppose if I wanted an orange I was going under the tree to pray that it would fall into my pocket? I just went up boldly and plucked what I wanted. And so the bread of heaven is offered to us, and all we've got to do is to go boldly up and take it. This is what God wants you to do. Everything is prepared for you.

There is a class, too, who say: "But I'm afraid I'll not hold out." How many people are stumbling over this! Now, if you come boldly up to the throne you'll get all the support you need—"Let us therefore come boldly unto the throne of grace, that we may obtain mercy and find grace to help in time of need."

There is a passage for you; that ought to be sufficient. And there is not a woman here today but can be kept, from this very day and this very hour, from evil—"For I, the Lord thy God, will keep you, without spot or wrinkle, and without blemish." Some of the vilest men who have ever trodden this earth have been saved with the grace of God. Some have been kept sixty or seventy years merely by the grace of God, and never wavered. "Come boldly to the throne of grace" and you will get power. That is sufficient. Won't you take him at his word? It seems to me that it is madness not to take the gift offered us by God.

Come to the Marriage

Let me call attention to another "come." My friends, the Bible is full of them, and you can't say if you don't come there have been no invitations. He says: "Come to the marriage." Now, you young ladies like marriages pretty well. Let a marriage come off in a church, and hundreds will be there; and probably next night, at the prayer meeting, there will scarcely be a dozen of you present. Now here is a marriage, and there is not a lady here whom God does not want to be present at the marriage feast. There is an invitation.

Come and Inherit the Kingdom

And here is another "come": "Come and inherit the kingdom prepared for you from the foundation of the world." God has got an inheritance for every one of you. The time will soon come, if you accept Christ and become as his bride, when you shall hear the voice of him saying to you: "Come and inherit the kingdom prepared for you from the foundation of the world." What a mistake it will be, my friends, if you will not hear that invitation given to you! There is an inheritance incorruptible in the heavens, a building not made with hands, and he wants everyone to enter into this inheritance, and so it is your privilege to be present at the marriage feast and receive the inheritance if you will.

Come Just as You Are

You know the first "come" in the Bible was given to Noah: God said, "Come thou, and all thy house into the ark," not a part of them, but "all thy house." That is the first "come" in the Bible, and all through that blessed book it is repeated; and now we come to the last one. It seems as if the Bible was created by this word "come." "The Spirit and the bride say come, and let him that is athirst come, and whosoever will, let him taste the water of life freely." There is our invitation, as broad as the world itself. And if God says you are to come, no power in heaven, or earth, or hell can stop you! He bids you come. Now bear in mind it is your sins God wants, and not your faith. You have nothing about you that he wants except your sins. People are continually trying to come to him by their faith, by their feelings, by their tears, by their good deeds, by their works; but you have to come to him just as you are. There is not a woman present but can roll off every sin and leave them in this tabernacle.

Now the question comes, What right have you to come? Why, because the King invites you. Suppose Queen Victoria had sent me an invitation to be present at Windsor at a feast given in honor of the marriage of one of her sons to a princess of Russia. I take the cars to New York, then the boat to Liverpool, then I would run down to London, where I would get the train to Windsor Castle. A sentry would be walking up and down in front of the gate. If I hadn't my invitation he would refuse me admittance; but there is not a soldier in the British army can keep me out, because I've got the Queen's invitation. But suppose the man looks at me and says, "You can't go into the presence of the Queen with those clothes; you are not fit to stand before the Queen." That is none of his business; that's hers. So the invitation comes from him, and he wants you to come and he will clothe you in garments fit for his presence. You will be stripped of every rag of self-righteousness, and a robe of spotlessness will be put upon you.

A great many people say, "I want to become clean before I come to Christ." Now, my friends, that is the devil's work. He tries to get people to believe that they can't come without getting rid of their sins; but as I've said, all through the Scriptures he bids you come as you are. We cannot take away our sins; come to him and he will blot them out.

A few years ago in London, there used to be a good many little children stolen to act as chimney sweeps. A child was stolen from a wealthy family, and a great reward was offered, but the child couldn't be found. One day he was sent up a chimney and came down on the other side, and into a beautiful room. The little fellow was bewildered. A lady was sitting there, and recognized him as her son, and although the boy was covered with dust, she ran to him, and drew him to her bosom. That is the way Christ will receive you. You needn't try to get rid of one particle of sin. He wants to save you as you are. "Whosoever will, let him come and drink of the waters of life freely." Will you come today? The Spirit and the bride invite you this afternoon.

What are you going to do with these loving invitations today?—"Come and hear," "Come and see," "Come and reason," "Come and rest," "Come and eat," "Come and dine," "Come and find grace," "Come unto the marriage," "Come and inherit the kingdom prepared for you from the foundation of the world," "Whosoever will, let him come." Ask God to help you to come today. If I were in your place I would settle this question before I left this building; I would press up to the kingdom of God and take him at his word. Join me in prayer that every soul in this building may come to Christ today.

Tekel

3

DANIEL 5:25

And this is the writing that was written,
MENE, MENE, TEKEL, UPHARSIN.

Our text for this evening is so short I am quite sure that those who have short memories can carry it away with them. Just listen to it; and if someone asks you after the meeting is over, I hope you will be able to repeat the text and its meaning.

In this short chapter of thirty-one verses we find everything that we know about Belshazzar. His history was very brief. We are told that he had a feast: he had a thousand of his noblemen, his lords, his mighty men, gathered there at Babylon. How long that feast lasted we are not told. Sometimes those Eastern feasts lasted for six months. We are also told that this young king was praising the gods of gold, of silver, of brass, of iron, of wood, and of stone.

All at once silence reigned in the banqueting hall. The king had sent out into the heathen temple, and had the golden vessels that had been taken from Jerusalem by his grandfather, Nebuchadnezzar, brought into that impious feast.

While they were rioting and drinking and carousing, judgment came suddenly and unexpectedly. And I think that if you will read the word of God carefully, you will find that judgment always comes suddenly and unexpectedly. While that feast was going on and all was merry, over on the wall, over the golden candlesticks, a hand could be seen and a finger writing the doom of that king.

Belshazzar sent for the wise men of Babylon to come and read the writing, offering the one who could translate the words a reward of great honor—namely, to be clothed in fine linen and in purple, to be given a golden chain around the neck, and to be made the third ruler in the realm. The wise men tried to read it, but they were not acquainted with God's handwriting.

That is the reason the skeptics and infidels can never understand the Bible—they don't know God's handwriting. With all the wisdom of the Chaldeans they could not make it out. They failed—utterly failed.

The king and all his lords were astounded. They never had seen such writing before. The Queen, however, knew of a man in the kingdom by the name of Daniel who, some fifteen years earlier, had told Nebuchadnezzar his dream and its interpretation. If Belshazzar would send for this prophet he might be able to read the handwriting on the wall. Consequently, Daniel was summoned and the king said to him: "If you read that handwriting and tell me what it is, I will give you great gifts, and I will make you the third ruler in the realm." You can imagine the scene as Daniel looked at the strange writing. Every eye was upon him. Then he said, "Let your gifts be to others, but I will read to you the handwriting." He knew God's writing. It was very familiar to him, and without any difficulty he read: "*Mene, mene, tekel, upharsin*." "What does it mean?" cried the king. Daniel answered, "*Mene, mene:* Thy kingdom is numbered and finished; *Tekel:* Thou art weighed in the balances, and art found wanting; and *Upharsin:* Thy kingdom is divided, and given to the Medes and Persians."

That very night Belshazzar's blood flowed with the wine in his banquet hall. That very night they could hear the enemy's army marching through the streets of Babylon. That very night Belshazzar's army was defeated, the men around the royal palace were driven back, Belshazzar was slain, and Darius the Mede took the throne.

It is not my object tonight to talk about a king who reigned twenty-five hundred years ago. I don't want to take you back that far. I want to bring my message to Cleveland, Ohio, if I can. I want to get into this audience tonight, and I want to ask every man and woman in this assembly, if you should be summoned into eternity at this hour, or at the midnight hour, what would be said: "Thou art weighed in the balances and found wanting"?

Weighed in God's Balances

The other night I preached from the text, "There is no difference," and I tried to *measure* our actions against the law. Tonight I propose to *weigh* them by the law. We find here this illustration of the balance used by God himself. *Tekel* means, "Thou art weighed in the balances and art found wanting." Let us imagine there were scales let down into this building—not of our making, for it is God who is going to weigh us; we are not going to weigh ourselves. The great trouble with most people is that they are trying to weigh themselves and they are making balances of their own. When we are weighed we are to be weighed in God's balances—not our own. The God who created us is going to weigh us. Let us imagine that the scales are fastened by a golden chain to the throne of God, who sits yonder in the heavens—a God of equity, a God of justice; and those balances come down tonight into this building, and here they are right before us, and every man, woman, and child in this assembly has to be weighed. Now, the question is, "Are you ready to be weighed?" A man begins to look around to his neighbors and other people, and says, "Yes, I am ready to be weighed. I am as good as the average." But that is not the way to look at it. What we want is to look at the law. We are to be weighed by the law of God. The God that created us has given us a law, and among all the skeptics and infidels that I have met, I have not found any that complained of that law. The trouble is not with the law. The trouble is with ourselves.

God's Law

Now, I have tonight some weights. You know when you go into a store to buy goods they take weights and weigh out your goods. Now, I have ten weights. I am going to put them in the balances, and I want this audience to come up and get in. As I put the weights in on one side, I invite each of you to come up and get in on the other side and see if you are ready to be weighed by the law of God.

The First Commandment

We will now put in the first weight: "Thou shalt have no other Gods before me." People who live in America think there is no such thing as idolatry. They think they have to go off into China, Japan or some heathen country to find idols. Don't flatter yourselves. We have idols in America. You have not got to go far to find them. You will find a thousand idolaters where you find one true Christian who worships the God of the Bible. Anything that a man considers more important than God is his idol. A man may make an idol of his wealth. A man may make an idol of his wife or his children. A man may make an idol of himself; a good many do that. They think more of themselves than of anything else in the wide world. They worship themselves. They revere themselves. They honor themselves. Self is at the bottom and top of everything they do.

Then there are a good many who worship the god of pleasure. Look at your young men today and your young ladies who bow down to the god of pleasure. "Give me a night in the ballroom and you may have heaven with all its glories. What do I care? Give me a night that will satisfy me in this world and I care nothing about the world to come." There are a good many gods. It would take all night to enumerate the gods you have here in Cleveland. There are a good many who bow down to the god of gold, that golden calf we read of in Aaron's day. "Give me money" is the cry of the world. "You may have the Bible with all its offers of mercy and heaven. You may have everything else if only you will give me money and a nice house on the avenue. That is all I ask for."

What is your god tonight? What do you think of most highly tonight? Oh, that the Spirit of God may wake us up. If we are trusting any idol, if we have some idol in our heart, may God tear it from us, because God says, "Thou shalt have no other gods before me." The sin of idolatry is one of the worst sins. In that Book there is more said against idolatry, perhaps, than any other sin. God will have the first place or none. Yet there are a great many people trying to give God the second place. They say, "Business has got to be attended to, I have got to attend to business, and if I have a little time after attending to business, I will attend to my soul's wants." Instead of giving the soul the first place they give the body and this life the first place. We take a good deal better care of our bodies than we do of our souls. You know that very well. Most people think a great deal more of this life than of the life to come. They think a great deal more of the gods around them than of the God of the Bible and the God of heaven.

The Second Commandment

The next weight is very much like the first. "Thou shalt not bow down thyself to any graven image or any likeness of anything that is in heaven above or that is in the earth beneath, or that is in the water under the earth." "Thou shalt not bow down to any image." I am not even to worship the cross or crucifix. I am not to bow down to anything but the God of heaven. I am not to worship any pictures, even if they are pictures of Jesus Christ. I think it is a great mistake that artists try to make pictures of the God of heaven and earth. It is a fearful thing. We are not to make any graven image of anything and then bow down to it.

The Third Commandment

But I must pass on rapidly. "Thou shalt not take the name of the Lord thy God in vain." Blasphemers come and be weighed. Step in and see how quickly the balance will kick the beam. If every blasphemer in this house was to be weighed tonight, what would become of our souls? "Thou shalt not take the name of the Lord thy God in vain." It is astonishing that those who blaspheme and curse God often say, "I don't mean anything by it." Well, God means a good deal when he says he "will not hold him guiltless that taketh his name in vain."

Profanity is one way of showing enmity to God. If God hadn't told man not to swear, I don't think he would have thought of it, but just because God said, "Thou shalt not swear," he wants to show his contempt for God by trampling his commandment under foot and spurning the grace of God. They say they can't help it. Yet these very men, when their mother is around, seldom swear. That shows they have more respect for their mother than they have for the God of heaven. If the wife happens to be around, or the children very often, they will not swear. Yet they will curse God, and swear to God's face—challenge God, as it were, to do his worst, and blaspheme. Yet when you talk to them about it they say, "Oh, well, I can't help it." It is false. Man may not of his own strength be able to turn from that sin, but God will give him grace. If a man has a new heart, he will have no desire to swear.

Those who are born of God will not want to take God's name in vain. Let the blasphemers in this house tonight remember that God is not going to "hold him guiltless that taketh his name in vain." If every blasphemer in this assembly should be cut down tonight with cursing and blasphemy upon his conscience and upon his heart, what would become of his soul? It is a fearful thing. You look upon a thief as a horrid monster, many of you, and you think he is a curse to the community, but is it not as bad to break God's laws as to break the laws of the state? You elect men to your legislature to make laws for you, and you think the laws which they make ought to be revered and honored more than the laws of high heaven. Here is a law from heaven, and that law says, "Thou shalt not take the name of the Lord thy God in vain." Yet we continue to show contempt for God and his laws and go right on blaspheming.

The Fourth Commandment

The next weight we will put in the balances is this: "Remember the Sabbath day to keep it holy." As it looks to me, we are drifting into a dark age. When we had slavery in this country, it was a great curse to the land—but we have something even worse today. No republic can exist without righteousness. If you teach men to break God's law, how long will it be before they will take their own laws into their own hands and tear them, as it were, to pieces and throw them to the winds and trample them under their feet?

Rather, we have to teach people to honor God's law if we expect them to honor the laws of our nation. We see this desecration of the Sabbath increasing every year, giving up a little here and giving up a little there. A few years ago in Chicago we did not have a theater open on the Sabbath, but now every theater is open. Every Sunday night those theaters are crowded. I want to say to the working men, if you give up the Sabbath, you give up the best friend you've got, and it will not be long before the capitalists will take your Sabbath and make you work seven days in the week, and you will not earn a dollar more than you do now in six days.

God is our friend; he would not have given us one day in seven unless it was for our good. We need it. Our animals need it. So let us honor the Sabbath day and keep it holy. If we have to give up some of our business, let us do it even if we don't make quite so much money. It is a good deal better for us to be right, to know we are honoring God, and to have God on our side, than it is to be breaking God's law. If a father teaches his child not to observe the Sabbath, takes him out riding on Sunday, teaches him not to go to the house of God, it will not be long before that boy will break his father's commandments. You teach him to dishonor God's law and he will dishonor yours. Is that not so? Does history not teach you that? Look around you. Have you got to go to the Bible to find that out? Is that not so? You take a man who goes around on the Sabbath, who doesn't teach his boy to go to Sabbath school and to church, but teaches him to play marbles, and it will not be long before that boy will break his father's heart—if he has a heart.

Throw this commandment into the balances and Sabbath-breaker, step in. If you do, what will become of you? You would find written on the wall, "*Tekel.* Thou art weighed in the balances and art found wanting." If a man cannot keep one day out of seven, what is he going to do with that eternal Sabbath in heaven? He will not want to go there. Heaven would be hell to him.

The Fifth Commandment

"Honor thy father and thy mother." That is another thing that shows we are drifting into a dark age. Men seem to be void of natural affection. Now, I want to call your attention to this fact: wherever you see a young man or young lady treating their parents with scorn and contempt, you can be sure that they will never prosper. I am not an old man and I am not a prophet, but I have lived long enough to notice that I have yet to find the first case where a young man or young lady has started out in life dishonoring father and mother, treating them with scorn and contempt, while also prospering. I believe today that one reason why so many are hedged in, unable to prosper, is because they have dishonored their parents. I do not know of anything that is more contemptible. I do not know of anything that sinks a man lower in my estimation, than to hear him speak disrespectfully of his father and mother, that cared for him in his childhood, that watched over him in sickness and did everything they could for him.

A young man that will go out and get drunk and come home at midnight, knowing his gray-haired mother is sitting up for him and weeping, is murdering her by degrees. I do not know why it is not just as bad to murder your father and mother, break their hearts and take months to do it and to kill them, as it is to take a revolver and shoot them down at once. I venture to say while I am talking here tonight some young man is in a brothel or some saloon or billiard hall, who will go home tonight or tomorrow morning beastly drunk, to curse the mother who gave him birth. Or perhaps some husband, having been untrue to his wife, will return home to bring his strong right arm upon her. How many murderers walk the streets today? I tell you truly, a young man who doesn't honor his father and mother, need not expect to prosper in this life, or in the life to come.

There was a fine looking young man. His father was a great drunkard, and his mother used to take in washing just to give that boy an education. She kept him at school and worked hard to do it. But one day he was out on the sidewalk talking with his mother. She had been washing and was not dressed as well as some ladies. He saw a school-mate coming towards him and he walked away from that mother. The school-mate asked him who that woman was he was talking to, and he said she was his washer-woman. Ashamed to own his own mother. You laugh, young lady. Shame on such a man as that. I think we ought to be ashamed of a man that would speak that way of a mother who is toiling day and night to give him an education.

"Honor thy father and thy mother." Treat them kindly; you will not always have them. By and by they will be gone. No one in the wide world loves you like that mother. No one in the wide world loves you like that father. Treat them kindly. Make the evening of their lives as sweet as you can. It will come back to bless you. But if you treat that father and mother with scorn and contempt, by and by, after a few years have rolled around you will be paid back in your own coin. "Be not deceived. God is not mocked. Whatsoever a man soweth that shall he also reap."

If there is a man or woman in this audience tonight that is not treating father or mother with respect or kindness, let him step into the balances and see how quick they will strike the beam. You will be found lighter than dust in the balances. You will find that word *Tekel* blazing out: "Thou art weighed in the balances and art found wanting."

The Sixth Commandment

"Thou shalt not kill." I suppose if you had said a few months ago to some of those men that have been killing lately that they were going to come to that, they would have said, "Am I a dog that I should do it?" They thought they would not; but when Satan takes possession of a man you don't know what he will do; you can't tell. When a man goes on step by step from one thing to another, it will not be long before he will be guilty of almost any crime. I have not got to kill a man to be a murderer. If I wish a man dead, I am a murderer at heart. If I get so angry with a man that I wish him dead, I am guilty in the sight of God. God looks at the heart, not at the outward man. We only look at the acts of men, but God looks down in the hearts. If I have murder in my heart, if I wish a man or woman dead, I am guilty.

"Thou shalt not kill." As I said before, there are a good many men who are not looked upon as murderers, that really kill their parents, kill their children, kill their wives. How many drunken men have murdered their wives! They have literally killed them inch by inch. They have gone to the altar and sworn before the God of heaven they would love, cherish, protect, and support that woman, and inside of five years they have become horrid monsters, and beaten that defenseless woman, until at last she has gone with a broken heart into the grave. Nothing but a cruel husband murdered that woman. "Thou shalt not kill." Do you think a God of judgment, a God of equity, a God of mercy will not bring those men into judgment?

The Seventh Commandment

We will put those six weights on the scale, and come to the next. I would pass over this commandment if I dared, but when I see what the enemy is doing, when I see the terrible, terrible state of things we are having all around, in all kinds of society, high and low, I feel that I must cry out and spare not. "Thou shalt not commit adultery." It is a sin that is not much spoken of. It is one of those things that we like to pass over. We hear a good deal about intemperance, but the twin sister of intemperance is adultery today. I want to read to you something that will express what I want to say, perhaps better than I can myself—the seventh chapter of Proverbs:

> 1 My son, keep my words, and lay up my commandments with thee.
> 2 Keep my commandments, and live; and my law as the apple of thine eye.
> 3 Bind them upon thy fingers, write them upon the table of thine heart.
> 4 Say unto wisdom, Thou art my sister; and call understanding thy kinswoman:
> 5 That they may keep thee from the strange woman, from the stranger which flattereth with her words.
> 6 For at the window of my house I looked through my casement,
> 7 And beheld among the simple ones, I discerned among the youths, a young man void of understanding,
> 8 Passing through the street near her corner; and he went the way to her house,
> 9 In the twilight, in the evening, in the black and dark night:
> 10 And, behold, there met him a woman with the attire of an harlot, and subtil of heart.
> 11 (She is loud and stubborn; her feet abide not in her house:
> 12 Now is she without, now in the streets, and lieth in wait at every corner.)
> 13 So she caught him, and kissed him, and with an impudent face said unto him,

[14] I have peace offerings with me; this day
have I payed my vows.
[15] Therefore came I forth to meet thee, dili-
gently to seek thy face, and I have found
thee.
[16] I have decked my bed with coverings of
tapestry, with carved works, with fine linen
of Egypt.
[17] I have perfumed my bed with myrrh,
aloes, and cinnamon.
[18] Come, let us take our fill of love until
the morning: let us solace ourselves with
loves.
[19] For the goodman is not at home, he is
gone a long journey:
[20] He hath taken a bag of money with him,
and will come home at the day appointed.
[21] With her much fair speech she caused
him to yield, with the flattering of her lips
she forced him.
[22] He goeth after her straightway, as an ox
goeth to the slaughter, or as a fool to the
correction of the stocks;
[23] Till a dart strike through his liver; as a
bird hasteth to the snare, and knoweth not
that it is for his life.
[24] Hearken unto me now therefore, O ye
children, and attend to the words of my
mouth.
[25] Let not thine heart decline to her ways,
go not astray in her paths.
[26] For she hath cast down many wounded:
yea, many strong men have been slain by
her.
[27] Her house is the way to hell, going
down to the chambers of death.

I want to say to the young people in this audience tonight, I do not know of a quicker way to ruin, I do not know of a quicker way down to hell, than the way of the adulterer. How a woman can surrender her virtue and take that road is one of the greatest mysteries of the present day, when they can look around and see how they have brought ruin and blight upon their life, and made it dark and bitter.

"Thou shalt not commit adultery!" I want to say to the libertines, those men who think they can commit adultery and cover it up, and think it never will come to light; some of them come to our public meetings; some of them come into our churches, and they sweep down the broad aisle, perhaps, with their wives upon their arms. They take the best seats, perhaps, in our churches, and they think the crime is covered up. Be not deceived. You ruin some man's daughter, and some vile wretch will ruin yours. You will find it out by and by.

Do you think that God is not going to bring men to judgment for this thing? Bear in mind that there is a God of equity sitting in the heavens, and this thing is going to become straight by and by. Not that the women are excused; one is as bad as the other. It is a sin, and it is a fearful sin. It is a sin we must cry out against at the present time. Don't let any adulterer or adulteress think he or she is going into the kingdom of God.

I want to say to the men here tonight, if you are bound to some fallen woman, if you are to-night guilty of that awful sin, give it up or give up heaven. If God should summon you into those balances tonight, what would become of you, vile adulterer, what would become of you? And you, poor, fallen woman!—you step in and see what would become of your soul. "Thou shalt not commit adultery!"

I want to say once more before I pass this commandment, that people may cavil and laugh and make light of it, as they do; but it is one of the greatest evils of the present day. Many a man's life is ruined, many a family has been broken up, and many a mother has gone down to her grave with a broken heart, because a son or a daughter has been ruined. It is a time that the church of God should send up one cry that our children should be kept. It is a day of temptation. It is a day of trial on our right hand and on our left. We are living in a day of decayed consciences.

But bear in mind that God will bring you into judgment by and by. Because sentence is not executed at once is no sign he is not going to execute the sentence. Paul reasoned with Felix "of righteousness, temperance, and *judgment to come.*" God has appointed a day when he will judge the world. Men may cavil and laugh as much as they like, but the day is appointed, the hour is fixed, and men have got to come to judgment, and then sins which you have committed in secret, and which you think are covered up, will come to light and be made public, unless they are covered by the blood of Christ; unless you repent and turn from them and ask God to have mercy upon you. They will be blazoned out to that great assembled universe.

The Eighth Commandment

"Thou shalt not steal." Is there a man here tonight that is a thief? Oh, no, you can say, there are no thieves here. Ah, don't you flatter yourself. There is many a man that thinks he is not a thief, that is a thief. When that young man takes twenty-five cents out of his employer's till to go to the theater, he is a thief as much as if he stole five thousand dollars and got caught. When a man appropriates to himself one dollar that belongs to someone else, he is a thief in the sight of God. A drop of water is water as much as Lake Erie is water; and the man that steals five cents is a thief in the sight of God as much as if he stole five hundred dollars.

Some men think that they are not thieves unless they get caught; and they think if they cover up their tracks and don't get caught they never will be brought to judgment. God's eyes are going to and fro through the earth. If you have a dollar that belongs to someone else, I beg of you, as a friend, to make restitution before you go to bed tonight. Pay it back if you want the light of heaven to flash across your path, if you want the smile and approbation of God to rest upon you, pay it back. You will not prosper as long as you have someone else's money. "Thou shalt not steal."

Now go to thinking. Have you anything that belongs to someone else? Have you cheated anyone? Have you jumped on to the horse cars and not paid your fare sometime when there was a great crowd and the conductor did not come around for it? That is stealing just as much as if you had been a defaulter or a forger. Have you been on the steam cars, and the conductor did not happen to come around and get your fare, and have you said, "I have got a ride for nothing"? You are a thief. You laugh at it, but it is not to be laughed at.

What we want today is righteousness in this nation. What we want in the church today above everything else is downright honesty; and may God give it to us! These things are not to be laughed at. Do you know how men become defaulters? Just in that way. They take a little to begin with, and conscience comes up and smites them. But the next day they take a little more, and their conscience doesn't trouble them so much. By and by they stifle conscience, and they can go on and do anything. That is the way these forgers begin. That is the way these defaulters begin. That is the way these great noted criminals begin. It is just the entering wedge. It is a little thing in their sight. But I tell you what we want to remedy is sin, and sin is not little.

If there is a man here tonight who has commenced a downward course, commenced a dishonest life, I want to beg of you tonight, before you sleep, make up your mind, God helping you, that you will straighten up any dishonesty of which you have been guilty, let it cost you what it will. Make restitution.

The Ninth and Tenth Commandments

"Thou shalt not bear false witness." I wish I had time to dwell on that, and the next: "Thou shalt not covet." There are the ten weights. Now, you cannot be weighed by one of them; you must be weighed by the whole. Is there a man or woman in this audience that is ready to be weighed? Come. I have heard so much about morals—is there a moral man here tonight? Are you ready? Have you not broken that decalogue? Is there a man or woman in this audience that has never broken any of these commandments? If you have broken one, you are guilty, for these are not ten different laws, but one law. If I have broken one of these commandments, I have broken the law of God, and I am guilty.

Let the moralist come up tonight and step into the scales, and see how quickly he will kick the beam. Bring on the moralist. See as he approaches the golden scales, he finds written on one side: "Except a man be born again he cannot see the kingdom of God." He says, "You will excuse me tonight, sir. I can't be weighed." He knows very well he will be found wanting. He knows very well it will be said, "*Tekel:* Thou art weighed in the balances and art found wanting." So he goes around to the other side of the scales and he sees written there, "Except ye be converted, and become as little children, ye shall not enter into the kingdom of heaven." "Well," he says, "I think I will not be weighed tonight." He is not quite ready to be weighed after all. So he goes around to the third side, and there he sees written: "Except ye repent, ye shall all likewise perish." He says, "I will not go in on that side." So he steps around to the fourth side, finding there the words written: "Except your righteousness shall exceed the righteousness of the scribes and Pharisees, ye shall in no case enter into the kingdom of heaven." "Well," he says, "I think I will not be weighed in these balances." But bear in mind God is going to weigh you in them. You have got to be weighed in them.

Let the rum-seller step up to the scales and see if he is ready to be weighed. As he steps up to those scales, he finds written there in golden letters: "Woe be to the man that putteth the bottle to his neighbor's lips." "Well," he says, "I think I won't be weighed tonight." He is not ready.

Let the drunkard come, rum bottle in hand. He looks at those scales and sees the words written: "No drunkard shall inherit the kingdom of God." He says, "I will not step in there tonight. I am afraid it will be found written on the wall, as it was on Belshazzar's wall: '*Tekel:* Thou art weighed in the balances, and art found wanting.'"

Is there a man here tonight that is ready to be weighed? I can imagine a man up in the gallery saying, "I wonder what Mr. Moody would do if he was to be weighed. I wonder if Mr. Moody is ready to step into those scales to be weighed." I want to tell you that I am; and I say it, I hope, without any boasting or egotism. You may put into the scales all those commandments, every one of them, and I am ready to step in against them. Do you want to know how? Here is how I shall do it. I will take Christ in with me. I took him as my Savior some twenty years ago. I am ready to step into those scales with him at any time. He will bring it down. He is our only hope. I would not dare to be weighed without him; but with him I am ready to be weighed at any time, day or night.

If God calls me to step into those scales tonight, I will step in; and I will step in with a shout, too; and I will not be looking on the wall to see if it is written "*Tekel:* Thou art weighed in the balances, and art found wanting," because Christ has kept the law, and I have got him. He offered himself to me, and I took him. He offers himself to every guilty sinner here tonight. To every man and woman who has broken that law, a Savior is offered, salvation is offered, and you can have it and live forever. But without Christ, what are you going to do?

What Think Ye of Christ?

MATTHEW 22:42

Jesus said, What think ye of Christ? Whose son is he? They said unto him, The Son of David.

I would like, if possible, to focus your attention tonight on that one question: What think ye of Christ? It is not what you think of the Bible. It is not what you think of this denomination or that denomination. It is not what you think of the church. It is not what you think of this preacher or that preacher, but "What think ye of Christ?"

The Teacher

I would like to have time to take him up tonight as a Teacher; the most wonderful teacher that ever came into this world. No man taught as he did. He did not teach like the Scribes and Pharisees. He taught as one who had authority. But that is not the object tonight.

The Preacher

I would like to have time to take him up as a Preacher. You talk about your great preachers, but this world never saw such a preacher as he was. He stood at the head of the list. There never has been, there never will be, another one like him. Very often ministers preach their opinions. He taught no opinions. He taught the truth, and it was so deep that the greatest theologians have not yet been able to fathom the depths of his teaching. Yet they were so simple and so beautiful that little children understood them, and they liked to hear him. In fact, there is not a book in the world that will interest children like the Bible. If you want a book that is full of beautiful stories for the children, that is the book.

Christ taught and preached the truth so that men could not forget it. There is not a prodigal on the face of this continent, in my opinion, who is not familiar with the fifteenth chapter of Luke. He drew that picture with such vividness and clarity that men cannot forget it. They know about that younger son; they know about that far country. And who can forget that story of the Good Samaritan? It kind of hooks into our memory. We can't get it out if we try.

I am told by travelers who have been through Palestine, that there is not a solitary thing you can see in that land that the Lord did not use as an illustration. The first parable he uttered was that of the sower. I can imagine, as he was teaching there upon the hillside, that he looked down the bank of that lake and saw a sower going forth in the spring to sow; and he said, "behold a sower!" and he drew a lesson his hearers couldn't forget.

There are four kinds of hearers. There are the wayside, the stony ground, the thorny ground, and the good ground hearers. Would to God there were more good ground hearers—hearers who would bring forth thirty, sixty, and a hundredfold. Those four kinds of hearers will remain. He taught the truth. Men cannot get around it. They may say there are not four kinds of hearers, but that doesn't make it so. Anyone who talks much to the public and mingles with them will find those kinds of hearers.

The Physician

I would like to talk to you about Christ as a Physician. Why, they say they have got some wonderful physicians in New York, in London, and in Paris. Their fame is known throughout all the country. But did you ever hear of a doctor that never lost a case? They say you have some very fine doctors here in Cleveland, but have you got one that never lost a case? Christ never lost a case. He had some pretty difficult cases, but he was a match for every case that came. Even if they were dead when he got there, they lived. He never preached any funeral sermons. A dead body would come to life when he came.

The Comforter

I would like to have time to take him up as a Comforter. As someone has said, he wiped away more tears in one day than all the infidels in eighteen hundred years. He has bound up more aching hearts, he has comforted more people, than all the infidels put together have ever done. He came for that purpose. "He sent me," Christ said, "to heal the broken-hearted." That is what he came for.

The Prophet

I have not come here tonight to take him up as a Prophet; not to speak to you about him as a Priest, or as a King. I have not come here to talk to you about him as a Preacher and a Teacher, or as a Physician, or as a Comforter. That is not the point tonight. I have got another point in view, and the point I want to call your attention to is this: Who was he? Was Christ what he claimed to be or not?

The God-Man

Now, I am one of those that contend that Jesus Christ was either God-man—he was both human and divine—or else he was a great impostor. Now you and I have great contempt for a man that is assuming to be more than he is. If a man tries to make you believe that he is a greater man than he is, he goes right down in our estimation.

Tonight I want to ask you to settle this question in your minds: Was Christ the God-man? Was he with God the Father before the world existed? He said he was. "Before Abraham was, I am." Now, this is a very important question. It is one of the most important questions that can come before us. We will not know how to treat Christ if we have not made up our minds who and what he is.

I was talking to a man not many hours ago, and he said it made no difference what he thought of Jesus Christ. I was pressing that point upon him. It makes all the difference in the world what we think of him. It is of very little account what you think of General Grant. It is of very little account what you think of the public men of this country today. It is of very little account what you think of Queen Victoria. It is of very little account what you think of the emperors and rulers of other nations. It is of little account what we think of other men in comparison with what we think of Jesus Christ.

The Question

This is *the* question; and I believe it is a proper question. I think I have a right as a preacher of the gospel to press this question home upon my audience; and I want those young men up in the gallery, I want every person in the house tonight, to put the question home to himself: "What do I think of Christ? What is my opinion of him?" We are very free to express our opinion about public men. There is hardly a person in this house that has not made up his mind about the public men of this nation. Jesus Christ is a public character, and we have a right to ask you what you think of him. There has been more written and more said about Jesus of Nazareth in your day and mine than of any hundred men that ever lived; and it is time for us to make up our minds what we think of him. Was he an impostor? Was he what some claimed him to be—a deceiver and a fraud? Or was he the God-man?

I am thoroughly convinced that we have got to take one side or the other. This idea that Jesus Christ was a very good man, as some people tell us, but he was only man, is false. It seems to me you could not utter a greater falsehood than that. If Jesus Christ was mere man, then he was guilty of one of the worst sins in the whole Bible. All through the Bible God has said, "Thou shalt have no other gods before me." But Christ said, "Come unto me all ye that labor and are heavy laden, and I will give you rest." He invites the world to come to him. Not only that, but he tells us that we cannot come to the Father except through him and by him. "I am the way." "I am the truth." "I am the life." "I am the resurrection and the life." That is what he says. Now, if that is not true, then he was an impostor, and if he was an impostor, he was rightly condemned and put to death. We ought to ratify the act of Calvary and own him as our Lord and our Master.

The Jury

Tonight I am going to ask you all to imagine that you are on a jury. Perhaps some of you ladies will say, "I never was in a jury box in my life." I suppose you never were, and perhaps there are a good many men here that never were in a court on a jury; but tonight I would like every one of you to keep your mind on the case we have before us. Let us examine a few witnesses and make up our minds on their testimony. If a man has a case in court he brings in witnesses. Both sides are brought in, and after they have heard the testimony on both sides, the members of the jury make up their minds.

Now, tonight I want to call in the witnesses, and we will just imagine that this is the witness box right here. Now, you know the worst enemies that Jesus Christ had while he lived on earth were the Pharisees and the Sadducees. They were constantly trying to entangle him. They were constantly trying to find something against him that they might put him to death. They made one attack after another and they failed. The most serious charge they could bring against him was this: "This man receiveth sinners and eateth with them." And it is a good thing that he does—for that includes us.

Caiaphas

Now, Caiaphas was president of the highest ecclesiastical court of that day. There was no higher tribunal. He sat in the place of Aaron. Jesus Christ was brought before Caiaphas. It was Caiaphas who gave the sentence of death. It was he who gave orders that Christ should be crucified. Now, suppose tonight we could bring that priest in here with his flowing robes upon him. Let him stand here, and let us ask him what he found against Jesus Christ. Let us ask him what Christ was guilty of, and let us hear what he says. He it was that put Jesus Christ under oath. You know if a man goes into court now, they make him hold up his right hand and solemnly swear that he will tell the truth, the whole truth, and nothing but the truth. Well, Caiaphas put Christ under oath. After the witnesses had come in and testified, then he put him under oath. "I adjure thee, by the living God, tell us plainly, art thou the Christ, the Son of the Blessed?" Christ said, "I am, and ye shall see me at the right hand of God, and coming in the clouds of heaven." "What further testimony do we want?" said Caiaphas. "We have heard blasphemy from his own lips." And he took his mantle and rent it, and said to the Sanhedrin, "What think ye?" And they said, "He is guilty of death." If Jesus Christ was not the God-man, then they ought to have put him to death, because there in that council he said, "I am," when the question was put to him, and he was under oath. It was that very thing that caused him to be put to death. It was his own testimony. He bore testimony to that very point—that he was the God-man; that he had come from heaven, and they should see him at the right hand of God, and coming in the clouds of heaven.

Pilate

But we have a good many witnesses to examine, and I will have to pass on. The next witness we want to bring into court is Pilate. Pilate was no Jew. He was put there by the Roman government to keep peace in that city. Now let us bring Pilate in here and examine him. The Jews brought Jesus before Pilate and Pilate examined him. And now hear what Pilate had to say after examining him and talking with him. This is his testimony: "I find no fault in him." If there could have been a flaw found in his character, do you think that Pilate would not have found it out in that blood-thirsty city? If there had been something wrong in his character; if he had been a fraud; if he had been a deceiver, do you think they would not have found it out? "I find no fault in this man. I will chastise him and let him go." "If you let him go, you are not Caesar's friend." Poor, vacillating Pilate. He did not have the moral stamina to live up to his conscience. So he sent Christ away to Herod, and Herod could find no fault in him.

Pilate's Wife

But we have another witness—a lady. We will bring in Pilate's wife. We have her testimony on record. She sent word to her husband, and this was her testimony: "Have thou nothing to do with that just man, for I have suffered many things this day in a dream because of him." People talk against Pilate now, but there are those a good deal worse than Pilate right here. They can find fault with Jesus Christ, but Pilate, that heathen governor, could find no fault with him. Pilate's wife could find no fault with him.

Judas

But here is another witness. Judas knew a good deal more about Jesus Christ than the witnesses that we have already seen in the witness box. Judas knew a good deal more about Jesus Christ than Caiaphas did. Perhaps Caiaphas never met Christ but once, and that on that memorable night when he was on trial. Pilate probably had never met him until he was brought before him. Pilate's wife had perhaps never seen him. But Judas had been with him for three years. He had heard those wonderful sermons. He had heard those wonderful parables. He had seen him perform those mighty miracles. He was with him when Lazarus came forth. Yet, he sold Christ for thirty pieces of silver. If there is anything against Christ he will certainly know it. Look at him! Look at the remorse! Look at the despair that has settled upon his countenance. Let him step into the witness box.

"Come now, Judas, tell us what you think of Christ. You have been with him for three years; you have been associated with him; you have been the treasurer of that little band. What think you of

Christ?" Hear him, as he throws down those thirty pieces of silver, "I have betrayed innocent blood." Even the very prince of traitors knew that Christ was innocent. That is what Judas thought of him. Men sit in judgment on Judas now; but how many men will say that Christ was not what he claimed to be. Judas knew it. "I have betrayed innocent blood." That is his testimony.

It is remarkable that every man that had anything to do with the death of Jesus Christ left his testimony. God made every one of them testify that his Son was innocent. Not one of them was permitted to speak against that Son. Their testimony has been put on record, and preserved and handed down to the present time.

The Centurion

If there is a criminal in this county that is to be executed, the sheriff has charge of the execution. The next witness we want to bring in is not a man that bore the name of sheriff, but really the man that held the same position that day—the centurion, who had charge of the execution. He was there at Calvary, and it was he who gave orders that those nails should be driven into his hands and his feet. It was he who gave orders that those soldiers should take that cross up and let it fall into that hole that had been dug.

So let the centurion be brought in here. Let him stand here in the witness box. "Come now, centurion, you had charge of that execution. You saw Jesus nailed to the cross. You saw him hanging between heaven and earth. What think you of that person? What think you of Jesus of Nazareth?" "Truly this was the Son God." That is what he said. He was convinced right then and there. That is what the sheriff said. Never was there such a scene on earth as that witnessed at the cross, when Jesus cried with a loud voice, "It is finished," and heaven took up the cry, and the rocks were rent, and the earth shook. This earth knew its Creator, although man did not, and the centurion was obliged to say, "Truly, this was the Son of God."

The Devils

But I have other witnesses. Do you know the testimony of the devils is on record? Their testimony has been put on record and kept for us. "Thou Son of the most high God, hast thou come here to torment us before our time?" Even the very devils knew him. And yet men don't know him; yet men don't think well of him; and there are men going up and down this nation talking against this Jesus, with all this testimony on record.

These were not friends of Jesus. These witnesses that we have been examining were among those who lifted up their voices against him. They were the bitterest enemies that he had.

But now we will bring in his friends. You know, if you want to get the truth of a case you want to hear both sides. We have heard from the enemies of Christ; and we have tried to be fair. We have brought in all the testimony that we can find. We challenge any skeptic or infidel to bring in any more testimony. Bring in your witnesses. Let them come and testify against the Son of God, if you can find them.

John the Baptist

"There was a man sent from God." That is the way it begins. I like that. He was sent to introduce this Christ. He was no fanatic, and he was not biased by the world. The world had no power over him. Flattery did not have any weight with him. Position did not have any weight with him. If he had been living now you would not find him up here on your fine avenues. He was one of the poorest of the poor. His food was that of locusts and wild honey. He did not wear a broadcloth coat. His coat was made of camel's skin, and he wore a leather girdle. But he came out on the banks of the Jordan and began to cry to that nation, "Repent, repent, for the kingdom of heaven is at hand!" And the nation began to be moved. Strange rumors went from town to town about this wonderful wilderness preacher, and thousands began to crowd to the banks of the Jordan to see him. What must have thrilled the audiences was that he said that he was just the forerunner of a coming One. One whose shoe latchet he was unworthy to unloose. He was just the herald of a coming One.

At last Jesus of Nazareth, the village carpenter, came down to the banks of the Jordan, and when John saw him he seemed to quail before him. He drew back and refused to baptize him. But the Lord commanded him, and he knew nothing but obedience—he did what the Lord told him to; and from that hour John, that mighty preacher, changed his text, and he had but one text after that: "Behold the Lamb of God that taketh away the sin of the world!" That was his cry. That is what he thought of him. John was just a mere guidepost, pointing toward him. He turned his disciples away from himself, and turned them toward his Galilean Prophet. "Behold the Lamb of God!" In another place he says, "I bear record this is the Son of God." "I must decrease, but he must increase." He began to preach down himself and preach up this wonderful Christ. I would take a long time to tell you what John thought of him. I cannot examine this witness as I would like to. It would take all night. I am afraid you would get weary.

Peter

We will take up another. Bring in Peter. We could not have a better witness, perhaps, than Peter. Peter denied him. Put Peter in the witness box, and say, "Well, Peter, you once denied this Christ and said you did not know him. You swore that you never knew him. Was that so, Peter?" I can see the tears trickling down his cheeks. "That is the greatest lie I ever told in my life. Know him! I think I do know him." "What do you think of him? What is your opinion of this Christ?" "God hath made this same Jesus whom ye have crucified both Lord and Christ." That is what he thought of him. As he stood there on the day of Pentecost, that was his testimony.

One day Christ seemed to be just hungering and thirsting for someone to confess him, and he said to his disciples around him: "Who do men say that I, the Son of Man, am?" "Some say you are Moses; some say you are Jeremiah; some say this prophet, some that prophet." "But who do you say I am?" "Thou art the Son of the living God," said Peter. "Blessed art thou, Simon Bar-jona; for flesh and blood never revealed that unto thee." Peter knew him. So when he preached on the day of Pentecost, he called him the Christ. "God hath made that same Jesus, whom ye have crucified, both Lord and Christ." "There is none other name under heaven given among men, whereby we must be saved."

The Thief

But let us call in that thief now. He was a notorious character. They punished only the most notable criminals by the death of the cross. That thief is a good witness. Let us bring him in. We are told by Matthew and Mark that those two thieves, when they went out that morning, from the prison to the cross, went out reviling, and when the crowd began to mock Christ, it says the two thieves also "cast it in his teeth." They, too, mocked. But all at once a strange thing takes place. The heart of one of these thieves seemed to be touched. I don't know what touched him, but I can imagine it was Christ's prayer, "Father; forgive them, for they know not what they do." That thief says, "He has a different spirit from what I have. He must be more than human. That must be the cry of the God-man." He seems to have been convicted right there. Hear what he says: "We indeed suffer justly, but this man hath done nothing amiss." That is what the thief thought of him.

Thomas

But here is Thomas. He has a good many descendants. Thomas belonged to the doubting school. There are a great many people like Thomas, doubting what they cannot see. They can't take things by faith. After the Lord had arisen, Thomas, like a good many people now, did not believe he had arisen, and I will venture to say Thomas was the most unhappy man in Jerusalem the first week after Christ came out of the sepulchre. That first Sunday, when he appeared to his disciples, Thomas was not there. They had a little prayer meeting, and he was missing. Perhaps he thought the whole thing was over, and that they would never hear of Christ again. But as Thomas walked down the street that Monday morning, whom should he meet but John. "Thomas, have you heard the news?" "What news?" "The Lord is risen." "Oh," said he, "I don't believe that. His spirit may have arisen, but his body is not." "Oh, yes, his body is. Why, I saw him last night, and I talked with him." "Oh, no, you must be mistaken; it must have been a vision." "Oh, I can't believe that."

Continuing down the street, Thomas had not got more than half a block before he ran into Peter. And Peter said, "Thomas, the Lord has risen indeed." "Oh, no, John just told me back there he had risen, but I don't believe a word of it." "Well," said Peter, "but I had an interview with him. He has forgiven me all my backslidings." "Oh, well, you just imagine you saw him. You must be mistaken. I don't believe he is risen at all." "Well, we went to the sepulchre, and it is empty. And there were two angels there and they said, 'Come, and see the place where the Lord lay,' and they said he had risen, and then afterwards we saw him." "Oh, well, I couldn't believe that. I couldn't believe it unless I see the prints of the nails in his hands, and put my fingers in them, and thrust my hand into his side." Poor Thomas. Before the week was over he has met more than a dozen who had seen Christ, but still he would not believe.

The church is full of Thomases today. They stay away from the prayer-meeting, where Christ meets his disciples, and they go out into the world and live among skeptics and infidels so much that they doubt everything from one end of the Bible to the other.

But the next Sabbath came, and Thomas was there that day; and while they were talking, and perhaps trying to convince Thomas that the Lord had risen, who should stand there but the Lord of Glory, and he said, "Thomas, reach hither thy hand and thrust it into my side, and put thy finger into these wounds." And Thomas cried out, "My Lord and my God!" That is what he thought of him. He owned him as his Lord and his God.

Oh, may God scatter our unbelief tonight, and may we say like Thomas, "My Lord and my God!" I don't want any other Lord but Jesus Christ. I don't want any other master but Jesus Christ. From that moment, Thomas never doubted that the Lord had come up out of the sepulchre.

John

But here is another witness. Ah, what a witness we have in John! He was a little nearer the heart of the Savior than any of the rest. He is that lovable disciple who laid his head upon the bosom of the Son of God. He heard the throbbing of that heart.

How he loved him. It would take all night to examine John, the beloved disciple. Oh, how much he thought of Christ! In the sight of John, he was the lily of the valley, the bright and morning star, the root and offspring of David. John said he was the light of the world. He says he was the life of the world. He says he was the resurrection and the life. It would take a good while to go through John. We would have to go all through his Gospel, then through the Epistles, and then through Revelation to find out what John thought of Jesus. Yes, he thought a good deal of him. If you want to get a good idea of Jesus, read what John wrote, you need not get any of these infidel books. Read John. John was with him all through his ministry. You could not have a better witness than John—that Galilean fisherman.

Paul

Here is another witness, and this witness ought to convince every skeptic. When I was in Baltimore, an atheist was persuaded to come into the meeting by some friend. Said he, "Just come in. I would like to have you come in. Of course you don't believe anything that is said, but just come in and see the audience." I happened to be preaching that night on this very subject, "What think ye of Christ?"

That atheist began to listen when I began to talk about Saul. "Now," said he, "I would like to hear what Saul has to say, because there was a time when Saul did not believe in him. There was a time when Saul was his bitterest enemy; and I would like to hear what that witness has to say." He listened, and thank God, he was convicted and converted, and I correspond with him now. He is one of the brightest lights in the whole city of

Baltimore. I hope there will be some atheist converted here tonight.

Now, let us hear what this little tentmaker of Tarsus has to say: "Paul, what think you of Christ?" Hear what he says: "I count all things but dung that I may win Christ." What did he care for this world? The fashion of it passes away. He had his eye fixed upon the Man on Calvary. He left the city of Jerusalem, where he was brought up, and where he held a high office. He left Gamaliel, and the whole of them, and he said, "The life which I now live in the flesh, I live by the faith of the Son of God, who loved me, and gave himself for me. Who shall separate us from the love of Christ? . . . I am persuaded that neither death, nor life, nor angels, nor principalities, nor powers, nor things present, nor things to come, nor height, nor depth, nor any other creature, shall be able to separate us from the love of God, which is in Christ Jesus, our Lord."

Yes, that little tentmaker thought a good deal of him! The moment he got a glimpse of the Man who died on Calvary his heart was taken captive. From the time Christ met him at Damascus until he met his death at Rome, he was all in all for Christ. Every hair in his head was true for Christ. Every drop of his blood was for Jesus Christ. Every time his pulse beat, it beat true to the Man that is at the right hand of God. If you want to find out what Paul thought of him, read some of his epistles. He thought everything of him. He thought nothing of himself. He had a good opinion of himself till he met Christ; but Christ was so much better than he was, that he sank down and was nothing. When a man sees Jesus Christ, he will have something then to feed upon. He will not think what a great man he is. He will think what a mean, contemptible wretch he is in comparison with the Man that is at the right hand of God.

Well, I have other witnesses. There are a good many that would like to come and testify. This Bible is full of them. I might call up Zacchaeus of Jericho. He could tell you a good deal about Christ. I might call up Mary Magdalene. She could tell you some wonderful stories about Jesus. I might call up Martha and Mary of Bethany, and their brother Lazarus. I would like to call up that man he met over there among the Gadarenes, out of whom he cast legions of devils. But we have no time to examine these witnesses. I think we have examined enough, haven't we? Isn't the jury satisfied that he was more than man; that he was God manifest in the flesh; that he was all he claimed to be?

The Angels

But if you will pardon me, I would like to call your attention to this: We have some unusual witnesses. The angels were once, and only once, permitted to bear witness. A friend was telling me earlier tonight that the angels do not have the privilege of coming down here and saving a soul to Christ. When Cornelius wanted to know the way of life, the angel had to tell him to send to Joppa, thirty miles away, and get Peter. But the angels had a chance once to tell what they thought of Jesus Christ. Those shepherds were, perhaps, half asleep there on the plains of Bethlehem, when all at once there came down a heavenly host all around, and the shepherds began to rub their eyes and look up. What a strain it must have been! What was it? Behold, I bring you good tidings of great joy, which shall be to all people. For unto you is born this day in the city of David a Savior, which is Christ the Lord." That is what the angels thought of him: "A Savior." And they burst out singing, "Glory to God in the highest, and on earth peace, good will toward men." Blessed gospel, my friends! Good tidings! Who will believe it tonight? Unto you—every soul in this house—unto you is born this day in the city of David a Savior. And now comes the question: What will you do with him?

Oh, let earth join with heaven tonight! Let all in this assembly join with that crowd around the throne, and let us say, "Worthy, worthy is the Lamb that was slain from the foundation of the world!" O poor, vile sinner, come out from the world and join the hallelujahs of heaven tonight, and let us all shout together, "Worthy, worthy is the Lamb!" Isn't he worthy? What do you ministers of the Cross say? Isn't he worthy? Let us up and publish it! Let us out and tell the world of him! The devil has been deceiving the world. The world does not know this Christ. And who shall publish him if we don't? The world is perishing for the want of Jesus Christ.

God the Father

God forbid that I should speak in any careless or any flippant way, but with all reverence let me say that there is one more witness that I want to bring in here tonight, and that is God the Father. As John stood on the banks of Jordan—and I can imagine there was an audience twice the size of this audience gathered around that wonderful preacher there on those banks as he held them breathless—when Jesus came forward and was baptized, as he came up out of that water there was a voice heard. Bible students tell us that the Jehovah of the Old Testament is the Christ of the New; and it is supposed by the best Bible students that for four thousand years, God the Father never broke the silence. From the time that Adam fell from the summit of Eden until Christ came at Jordan, God the Father had not broken the silence. But it is written in the Book that he came to do God's will, and the moment he began his ministry God broke the silence of four thousand years. As Jesus came up out of the water a voice was heard saying, "This is my beloved Son in whom I am well pleased." Oh, if God is well pleased with him, let us be pleased with him. If the God of heaven is well pleased with Jesus, let us be pleased with him.

On the Mount of Transfiguration, when Peter wanted to build three tabernacles, one for Moses, one for Elias, and one for Christ, putting Christ on a level with Moses and Elias, God Almighty came in a cloud and snatched Moses and Elias away, and left Christ alone, and he broke the silence again: "This is my beloved Son in whom I am well pleased. Hear ye him."

Oh, may we hear the voice of the Son of God tonight calling us from the world and from ourselves, and may we think well of him! Oh, let us think well of Christ, and let us go out and publish his name, and proclaim salvation to a perishing world!

The Death of Christ 5

ISAIAH 53:4–5

Surely he hath borne our griefs, and carried our sorrows; yet we did esteem him stricken, smitten of God, and afflicted. But he was wounded for our transgressions, he was bruised for our iniquities; the chastisement of our peace was upon him; and with his stripes we are healed.

Five times in our text the little word "our" is used: *our* sorrows, *our* griefs, *our* iniquities, *our* transgressions, and the chastisement of *our* peace. There is a substitute for you! I would like, if I could, to make the fifty-third chapter of Isaiah real for each one of us tonight. I would like, if I could, to bring before us this truth: that Christ has suffered *for each one of us*. We take up the Bible, we read the account of his crucifixion and death, how he suffered in agony; and we lay the Bible down, go away, and think nothing more about it.

When the war was raging, I would read about one of its great battles having been fought, where probably thousands of soldiers had been killed or wounded. Yet, after reading the article, I would lay the paper aside and forget all about it. Later, when I went into the army myself, I saw the dying men. I heard the groans of the wounded. I helped to comfort the dying, and bury the dead. I saw the scene in all its terrible realities. After I had been on the battlefield, I could not read an account of a battle without it making a profound impression upon me.

I wish I could bring before you in living colors the sufferings and death of Christ. I do not believe there would be a dry eye here. I speak of his physical suffering, of course, for no one can know what Christ's mental sufferings were. When a great man dies, we are all anxious to get his last words; and if it is a friend, how we treasure up that last word—how we tell it to his friends! We never tire of talking to our loved ones of how he made his departure from the world. Now let us visit Calvary.

Jerusalem

Let us go back in our imagination to the time of Christ's crucifixion, and suppose we are living in the city of Jerusalem and walking its streets. On the final Tuesday Christ spent with his disciples before he was crucified, we see people running down the streets. As we get nearer and enter with the others into one of Jerusalem's houses, we find Jesus with his disciples. We can see sorrow depicted upon Christ's brow. His disciples see it also, but do not know what has caused his grief.

Our Lord's last hours must have been a great mystery to the twelve disciples. He had filled Jerusalem with wonder at the resurrection of Lazarus; yet here he was talking about death. What did it mean?

> And as they did eat, he said, Verily I say unto you that one of you shall betray me. And they were exceedingly sorrowful; and began every one of them to say unto him, Lord, is it I? And he answered and said, he that dippeth his hand with me in the dish, the same shall betray me. The Son of Man goeth as it is written of him: but woe unto that man by whom the Son of Man is betrayed! It had been good for that man if he had not been born. Then, Judas, which betrayed him, answered and said, Master, is it I? He said unto him, thou hast said.

Following Christ's words to Judas, "What thou doest do quickly," Judas left the room. For three years he had been associated with the Son of God. For three years he had sat at the feet of Jesus. For three years he had heard those words of sympathy and love that had fallen from his lips. For three years Judas had been one of "the twelve." He had seen Jesus perform his wonderful miracles; he had heard the parables as they fell from the lips of the Savior. For three years he had seen what the prophets would have been glad to see; he had been exalted to heaven with privileges. Yet, Judas went out into the night—the darkest night that this world has ever seen—the saddest parting that ever took place on this earth. He went out into darkness, despair, remorse, and death. See him as he goes down those steps, off into the darkness and blackness of the night! He went to the Sanhedrin, and to the chief priests, "and said unto them, What will ye give me, and I will deliver him unto you? And they covenanted with him for thirty pieces of silver."

The Selling of Jesus

What a small amount! We condemn Judas; but how many of us are selling Christ for even less than he did! How many give him up, and with him all hope of heaven, for less than thirty pieces of silver! There are men who will sell him for a little pleasure, and women who will sell him for two or three hours in a ballroom!

Hear the money being counted. Judas put it into the bag, and said, "Give me a band of men, and I will take you where he is."

That same night Jesus said to his disciples:

> Let not your heart be troubled: ye believe in God, believe also in me. In my Father's house are many mansions: if it were not so, I would have told you. I go to prepare a place for you. And if I go and prepare a place for you, I will come again, and receive you unto myself; that where I am, there ye may be also.

Instead of the disciples trying to comfort Jesus, he sought to cheer them. Taking his disciples "unto a place called Gethsemane," he told them: "Sit ye here, while I go and pray yonder." And he took with him Peter and the two sons of Zebedee, and began to be sorrowful and very heavy. Then spoke he unto them: "My soul is exceeding sorrowful, even unto death: tarry ye here, and watch with me." And he went a little farther, and fell on his face, and prayed, saying, "O my Father, if it be possible, let this cup pass from me! Nevertheless not as I will, but as thou wilt."

Returning to the disciples, he found them asleep. "What, could ye not watch with me one hour? Watch and pray, that ye enter not into temptation: the spirit indeed is willing, but the flesh is weak."

Leaving a second time, he continued to pray: "O my Father, if this cup may not pass away from me, except I drink it, thy will be done." And he returned to find them asleep again, for their eyes were heavy. So he left them and went away again, praying a third time, saying the same words.

Then returning to his disciples, he said unto them, "Sleep on now, and take your rest: behold, the hour is at hand, and the Son of Man is betrayed into the hands of sinners. Rise, let us be going: behold, he is at hand that doth betray me."

He who knew no sin was to bear all our sins. He who was as spotless as the angels of heaven was to suffer for us. From this lone spot his earnest prayers ascended to heaven.

The Arrest

Finally, those also who were hunting for him arrived—peering through the olive trees. Approaching those who had come to arrest him Jesus asked: "Whom seek ye?" They answered: "We seek Jesus of Nazareth." "I am he," he responded.

Something about that reply terrified those who had come. They trembled, and fell to the ground. Then Judas came up and kissed him. When Judas had kissed Christ, the soldiers seized him; for Judas had told them that when they saw him kiss a man, that was he. Those hands that had wrought so many wonderful miracles, those hands that had often been raised to bless the disciples, were bound. Then Peter drew his sword and cut off the ear of the high priest's servant. Jesus healed the wound at once. He would not let the man suffer. He did not come to destroy life, but to save it.

Then they took him back to Jerusalem. We can see the soldiers and the populace mocking him. They led him away to Annas first, for he was father-in-law to Caiaphas, the high priest; and from Annas he was sent to Caiaphas.

Then the high priest questioned Jesus about his disciples and his doctrine. Jesus answered: "I spake openly to the world; I taught in the synagogue, and in the temple, whither the Jews always resort; and in secret have I said nothing. Why askest thou me? Ask them which heard me, what I have said unto them: behold, they know what I said." And when he had thus spoken, one of the officers who stood by struck Jesus with the palm of his hand, saying, "Answerest thou the high priest so?" Jesus answered him, "If I have spoken evil, bear witness of the evil: but if well, why smitest thou me?"

Christ before the Rulers

After this they led him before the Sanhedrin, the rulers of the Jews. There were seventy that belonged to that Sanhedrin. Since the law required that two witnesses must appear against a person on trial before he could be convicted, two witnesses were found and brought before the body to give their false testimony. Then the high priest asked Jesus to respond to their accusations, but he said nothing. The high priest asked him a second time, "Art thou the Christ, the Son of the Blessed?" Jesus answered, "I am; and ye shall see the Son of Man sitting on the right hand of power, and coming in the clouds of heaven." Then the high priest said, "What need we of any further witnesses? Ye have heard the blasphemy: what think ye?" And the verdict came forth: "He is guilty of death!"

What a sentence! Pronounced guilty of death! You can see one of the soldiers strike him with the palm of his hand. Another spit in his face. Then he was imprisoned. His disciples left him. Peter swore he didn't know him. Judas returned to throw down the money that had been paid him for betraying innocent blood, and went out and hanged himself.

In the morning, they took Jesus to the hall of judgment to appear before Pilate. "What accusation bring ye against this Man?" Pilate asked. They answered and said unto him, "If he were not a malefactor, we would not have delivered him up unto thee." Then said Pilate unto them, "Take ye him, and judge him according to your law." The Jews therefore said unto him, "It is not lawful for us to put any man to death." Then Pilate entered into the judgment hall again, and said to Jesus, "Art thou the King of the Jews?" Jesus answered him, "Sayest thou this thing of thyself, or did others tell it thee of me?" Pilate answered, "Am I a Jew? Thine own nation and the chief priests have delivered thee unto me: what hast thou done?" Jesus answered, "My kingdom is not of this world: if my kingdom were of this world, then would my servants fight, that I should not be delivered to the Jews: but now is my kingdom not from hence."

While all these things were taking place, Jerusalem was filled with strangers from all parts of the country. They had heard that the Galilean prophet had been brought before the Sanhedrin, that they had condemned him, and that he was to die the cruel death of the Cross. All that remained was the securing of Pilate's consent.

But Pilate said, "I find no fault in this man. I will chastise him, and let him go." But they shouted, "If you let him go, you will not be Caesar's friend, for he has stirred up the country from Galilee to here." "Why," said Pilate, "is he a Galilean?" And they told Pilate that he was from Nazareth. When he heard that, he was glad to get rid of the responsibility—and said, "Then I will send him to Herod."

A great many Roman soldiers were there to control the crowds in the streets, much as our police do today. You can see these soldiers going before the crowd that have Jesus, clearing the streets.

Herod was glad when Jesus was brought into his presence, for he hoped that he would perform some miracle to gratify his curiosity. We are told that Herod's men of war set him at naught. They said, "Hail, King of the Jews!" Then they came up, and struck him on the face. Let us make the scene real today! "He was bruised for our transgressions."

After they mocked him, they again dressed him up in his own garments and brought him before Pilate. You can see the crowd around the judgment hall. They are ready to put Christ to death. Indeed, all classes of persons conspired to crucify him. "The kings of the earth stood up, and the rulers were gathered together against Jehovah, and against his Christ." The dissolute, blood-thirsty Herod; the crafty, worldly-minded Pilate; the idolatrous Gentiles; and the religious people of Israel—all united to condemn to death God's holy Child, Jesus.

Jesus or Barabbas?

Struck by a new thought, Pilate remembered that it was a custom among the Jews that on a certain day one prisoner was to be released to them, and to go unpunished. So he said to the Jews: "Which of these two prisoners shall I release, Jesus or Barabbas?" When they found out what was going on, the enemies of Christ went through the crowd and asked that Barabbas might be released. "Which shall I release unto you, Jesus or Barabbas?"—Jesus who raised the dead, or Barabbas who took the lives of men, whose hands were dripping with the blood of his fellow men? No sooner was the question put to the crowd than they lifted up their voices, shouting: "Barabbas! Barabbas!" Then he asked, "What shall I do with Jesus?" And the cry rang through the streets from those who but a few days before had shouted "Hosanna, son of David": "Let him be crucified!" When the governor heard it, he turned and washed his hands, saying: "I am innocent of the blood of this just person."

I never knew until lately what the Roman custom of scourging was. When I first read about it I could not help but weep, and ask Christ to forgive me for not having loved him more. Let us imagine the scene when he is taken by the Roman soldiers to be scourged. The orders were to put forty stripes, one after another, upon his bared back. Sometimes it took fifteen minutes, and the man died while being scourged. See him stooping while the sins of the world are laid upon him, and the whips come down upon his bare back, cutting clear through the skin and flesh to the bone. After they had scourged him, instead of pouring oil into the wounds of him who came to bind up the brokenhearted, they dressed him up again, and some cruel wretch reached out to him a crown of thorns, which was placed upon his brow. The Queen of England wears a crown of gold, filled with diamonds and precious stones, worth millions; but when they came to crown the Prince of heaven, they gave him a crown of thorns, and placed it upon his brow; and in his hand they put a reed for a scepter.

> And the soldiers led him away into the hall, called Praetorium; and they called together the whole band. And they clothed him with purple, and platted a crown of thorns, and put it about his head, and began to salute him, Hail, King of the Jews! And they smote him on the head with a reed, and did spit upon him, and bowing their knees worshiped him. And when they had mocked him, they took off the purple from him, and put his own clothes on him, and led him out to crucify him.

Calvary

Through the gates of the city bursts the crowd. Two thieves are brought for execution. Between the two thieves is the Son of God, carrying his cross. Ladies often wear small crosses made of gold, and wood, and stone, around their necks; but the cross that the Son of God carried was a heavy tree, made into a cross. I can see him reeling and staggering under it. Having lost so much blood, he was too faint to carry it and it well-nigh crushed him to the earth. And the crowd hooted: "Away with him! Away with him!"—a pestilent fellow, as they called him.

They arrived at Calvary a little before nine. Then they took the Son of God, and laid him out upon the cross. I can see them binding his wrists to the arms of the cross. After they had got him bound up, a soldier pounded a nail into the palm of his hand with his heavy hammer, driving it down through the bone and flesh and into the wood. Then they fastened the other hand. Then they brought a long nail for his feet. The soldiers then gathered round the cross and lifted it up, and the whole weight of the Son of God came upon those nails in his hands and feet.

Come with me and look at those wounds! Remember that crown of thorns laid upon his brow by a mocking world. Look at him as he hangs there. Observe the people who pass by deriding him! Listen to the thief say, "Save us, and save thyself, if thou be the Son of God."

The Cross

But hark! Christ, who has not spoken since he uttered those words of comfort to the daughters of Jerusalem, at last utters a cry from the cross. What is it? Is it a cry to God to take him down from the cross? Is it a cry of vengeance? Or is he calling fire down on them? No! He cried: "Father, forgive them; for they know not what they do!" Was there ever such love as that? While they were crucifying him, he was lifting his heart to God in prayer. His heart seemed to be breaking for those sinners. How he wanted to take them in his arms! How he wanted to forgive them!

At last he cried, "I thirst!" Instead of giving him water from one of his own springs, however, they gave him a draught of gall mixed with vinegar. It was about the only thing he ever asked for in the world, and you see how they treated his request.

There he hung! You can see those soldiers casting lots for his garments, as they crowd around the foot of the cross. The crowd continued to mock and deride and make all manner of sport of him. His response was: "Father, forgive them; for they know not what they do!"

We have seen what Christ suffered physically; but his mental sufferings were too deep for any mortal man to understand. He was dying in the sinner's stead, with the sins of the world upon his head. A righteous God could not look upon sin, even when borne by the eternal Substitute; and he hid his face from him. Earth had cast him out, man had mocked and rejected him; his own disciples had forsaken him and fled; and now even his Father would not look upon him. It well nigh broke our Savior's heart, and in the bitter anguish of his soul, he cried: "My God, my God, why hast thou forsaken me?"

In the midst of this darkness and gloom there came a voice from one of those thieves. It flashed into his soul as he hung there, "This must be more than man; this must be the true Messiah!" He cried out, "Lord, remember me when thou comest into thy kingdom!" Here was the last act of Jesus—snatching the thief from the jaws of death, saying: "This day shalt thou be with me in Paradise."

We are anxious to get the last word or act of dying friends. And here are his words: "It is finished." Salvation was wrought. Atonement was made. His blood had been shed. His life had been given. Undoubtedly, if we could, we would have seen legions of devils hovering around the cross.

The dark clouds of death and hell came surging up against the bosom of the Son of God, and he drove them back—much as you have seen when the waves come gathering up and surging against the rock, only to recede and return again. The billows went over him. On the cross, he was conquering death, and Satan, and the world. And he was treading the wine-press alone.

"It is finished!" Perhaps no one who heard it knew what it meant. But the angels in heaven knew. I can imagine the bells of heaven ringing out, and the angels singing, "The God-man is dead! Full restitution has opened the way back into Paradise, and all man has to do is to look and live!"

After he cried, "It is finished!" He bowed his head, commended his spirit to God, and gave up the ghost. Do you tell me you see no reason why you should love such a Savior? Have you no desire to receive him, and become his?

Some time ago, a prominent physician of Denver, Colorado, was called to attend a patient in the last stages of what appeared to be consumption, but which upon examination proved to be simply a wearing away of life—a decay of the energies of mind and body. Although well supplied with money, the stranger was seemingly without friends or relatives. He wrote no letters, and received none. An alien to the tenderness and charities which sanctify the affections, he seemed to be drifting out of the world, in which, for him, all the flowers of the heart had perished—a bleak and desolate old man, hastening out of the sunshine into the winter of the grave.

After making a thorough examination of the case, the doctor told him that although he could find no organized disease, yet he was dying. "I know it," replied the patient. "But have you no idea of what brought you to this plight?" inquired the interested man of science. "It is curious. You have heard a great deal about cases like mine—more as an exaggeration of the fancy than as an actual occurrence; but strange as it may appear, I am dying, as you say—of a broken heart." "You surprise me!" answered the physician. "Yes, I surprise myself. I did not come to your health-giving climate as others do, in search of a longer lease of life, but to die in peace, and alone."

"But have you no friends?" asked the doctor. "None that I can claim. My past is sealed with the shadow of a crime, and over my nameless grave not even a memory must hover. I am already dead to all who ever knew my name!" "You say you are a criminal?" pursued the doctor. "No, I am none. But I assume the stigma to shield another." "And that other?"

"It is my son," said the patient. "What was the nature of the crime?" inquired the physician, his curiosity getting the better of his prudence. The shadows of twilight were falling around them. Through the open window streamed the soft brilliance of the dying day. Clouds of amethyst and purple floated lazily on the far-off hill. But in the chamber where the fevered breath was drawn quick and short, there was a hushed stillness which seemed in keeping with ghostly shadows. "It was murder," said the man.

"It was fixed on you?" asked the doctor. "Yes, on me. I assumed it, and then escaped—not to evade the vengeance of the law, but to spare him I loved the stigma of a felon's death."

"How long ago was this?" continued the physician. "Twelve years," said the man. "And you have been a wanderer ever since?" "Ever since."

The feeble pulse was fluttering, the shattered form was growing rigid momentarily. "Will you tell me no more?" whispered the physician. "It is all I have to tell!" said the man. The next instant he was dead. He had kept his secret, and sacrificed his life in keeping it.

What should we think of that son, if we knew that he did not cherish and treasure as his dearest possession the memory of this loving, self-sacrificing father? Could we imagine such base and heartless ingratitude? Surely not. Yet the sacrifice that father made on behalf of his boy was as dust on the balance compared with the life of humiliation, of pain, and sorrow, and shame, voluntarily chosen and endured by our blessed Lord; with his mental anguish and bloody sweat in the garden; with his bodily sufferings and brutal treatment on the cruel cross; with the unspeakable burden of human sin that was laid upon him, and that he gladly bore, that he might redeem a lost rebellious world.

Shall we render him no return? Shall we banish such love from our hearts? Shall he not see the travail of his soul, and be satisfied, as he lives in the deepest heart's affection of those whom he loved, and for whom suffered and died? Oh, the height and the depth of our ingratitude and infamy if we scorn the love of such a Savior, and if we do not exalt him to his rightful place, as King in our hearts and lives! God forbid that one soul who has ever heard the story of the Cross should be guilty of these things.

Thank God, Christ is not now on the cross or in the tomb. He has risen, and now sitteth at the right hand of the Father, where he waits to bless his believing people and to receive them into his presence and glory.

Christ All and in All 

COLOSSIANS 3:11

Where there is neither Greek nor Jew,
circumcision nor uncircumcision,
barbarian, Scythian, bond nor free:
but Christ is all, and in all.

Christ is *all* to us that we make him to be. I want to emphasize the word *all*. Some men make him to be "a root out of a dry ground," "without form or comeliness." He is nothing to them; they do not want him. Some Christians have a very small Savior, for they are not willing to receive him fully, and let him do great and mighty things for them. Others have a mighty Savior, because they make him to be great and mighty.

Christ Our Savior

If we would know what Christ wants to be to us, we must first of all know him as our Savior from sin. When the angel came down from heaven to proclaim that he was to be born into the world, you remember he gave his name, "He shall be called Jesus, for he shall save his people from their sins." Have we been delivered from sin? He did not come to save us *in* our sins, but *from* our sins. Now, there are three ways of knowing a person: Some you know only by hearsay; others you know only slightly; and others you know intimately. So I believe there are three classes of people today in the Christian Church and out of it: those who know Christ only by reading or by hearsay; those who have a slight personal acquaintance with him; and, those who, like Paul, "know him and the power of his resurrection." The more we know of Christ the more we shall love him, and the better we shall serve him.

Let us look at him as he hangs upon the Cross, and see how he has put away sin. He was manifested that he might take away our sins; and if we really know him we must first of all see him as our Savior from sin. You remember how the angels said to the shepherds on the plains of Bethlehem, "Behold, I bring you good tidings of great joy, which shall be to all people: for unto you is born this day, in the city of David, a Savior, which is Christ the Lord." Then if you go clear back to Isaiah, seven hundred years before Christ's birth, you will find these words: "I, even I, am the Lord; and beside me there is no Savior."

And again, in the First Epistle of John, we read: "We have seen, and do testify, that the Father sent the Son to be the Savior of the world."

All the heathen religions, we read, teach men to work their way up to God; but the religion of

Jesus Christ is God coming down to save us, to lift us up out of the pit of sin. In Luke, we read that Christ himself told the people what he had come for: "The Son of Man is come to seek and to save that which was lost." So we start from the Cross, not from the cradle. Christ has opened up a new and living way to the Father; he has taken all the stumbling-blocks out of the way, so that every man who accepts of Christ as his Savior can have salvation.

Christ Our Deliverer

But Christ is not only a Savior. Even I might save a man from drowning or rescue him from an untimely grave. It is unlikely, however, that I could do any more for him. Christ is more than a Savior. When the children of Israel were placed behind the blood, that blood was their salvation; but they still heard the crack of the slave-driver's whip and they still needed to be delivered from the Egyptian yoke of bondage. Then it was that God delivered them from the hand of the Pharaoh. I have little sympathy with the idea that God comes down to save us, and then leaves us in prison, the slaves of our besetting sins. No; he has come to deliver us, and to give us victory over our evil tempers, our passions, and our lusts. Are you a professed Christian but one who is a slave to some besetting sin? If you want to get victory over that temper or that lust, go on to know Christ more intimately. He brings deliverance for the past, the present, and the future. He is the one "who delivered; who doth deliver; who will yet deliver."

How often, like the children of Israel when they came to the Red Sea, have we become discouraged because everything looked dark before us, behind us, and around us, and we did not know which way to turn. Like Peter, have we not said, "To whom shall we go?" But God has appeared for our deliverance. He has brought us through the Red Sea right out into the wilderness, and opened up the way into the Promised Land.

Christ Our Redeemer

But Christ is not only our Deliverer; he is our Redeemer. That is something more than being our Savior. He has brought us back. "Ye have sold yourselves for nought; and ye shall be redeemed without money. We were not redeemed with corruptible things, as silver and gold." If gold could have redeemed us, could he not have created ten thousand worlds full of gold?

Christ Our Way

When God had redeemed the children of Israel from the bondage of Egypt, and brought them through the Red Sea, they struck out for the wilderness; and then God became to them their Way. I am so thankful the Lord has not left us in darkness as to the right way. There is no living man who has been groping in the darkness but may know the way. "I am the Way," says Christ. If we follow Christ we shall be in the right way, and have the right doctrine. Who could lead the children of Israel through the wilderness like the Almighty God himself? He knew the pitfalls and dangers of the way, and guided the people through all their wilderness journey right into the promised land. It is true that if it had not been for their accursed unbelief they might have crossed into the land at Kadesh Barnea, and taken possession of it, but they desired something besides God's word; so they were turned back, and had to wander in the desert for forty years. I believe there are thousands of God's children wandering the wilderness still. The Lord has delivered them from the hand of the Egyptian, and would at once take them through the wilderness right into the Promised Land, if they were only willing to follow Christ. Christ has been down here, and has made the rough places smooth, and the dark places light, and the crooked places straight. If we will only be led by him, and will follow him, all will be peace, and joy, and rest.

In the frontier, when a man goes out hunting he takes a hatchet with him, and cuts off pieces from the bark of the trees as he goes along through the forest: this is called "blazing the way." He does it that he may know the way back, as there is no pathway through these thick forests. Christ has come down to this earth and has "blazed the Way": Now that he has gone up on high, if we will but follow him, we shall be kept in the right path.

I will tell you how you may know if you are following Christ or not. If someone has slandered you, or misjudged you, do you treat them as your master would have done? If you do not bear these things in a loving and forgiving spirit, all the churches and ministers in the world cannot make you right. "If any man have not the Spirit of Christ, he is none of his." "If any man be in Christ Jesus he is a new creature: old things are passed away; behold, all things are become new."

Christ Our Light

Christ is not only our way. He is the Light upon the way. He says, "I am the Light of the world." He goes on to say, "He that followeth me shall not walk in darkness, but shall have the light of life." It is impossible for any man or woman who is following Christ to walk in darkness. If your soul is in the darkness, groping around in the fog and mist of earth, let me tell you it is because you have got away from the true light. There is nothing but light that will dispel darkness. So let those who are walking in spiritual darkness admit Christ into their hearts: he is the Light. I call to mind a picture which at one time I esteemed highly but would not now have in my house unless its face was turned to the wall. It represents Christ as standing at a door, knocking, and having a big lantern in his hand. Why, you might as well hang up a lantern to the sun as put one into Christ's hand. He is the Sun of Righteousness; and with him it is our privilege to walk in the light of an unclouded day.

Many people are searching for light, and peace, and joy. We are nowhere told to seek after these things. If we admit Christ into our hearts these will all come by themselves. I remember, when I was a boy, I used to try in vain to catch my shadow. One day I was walking with my face to the sun; and as I happened to look around I saw that my shadow was following me. The faster I went the faster my shadow followed; I could not get away from it. So when our faces are directed to the Sun of Righteousness, the peace and joy are sure to come. A man said to me some time ago, "Moody, how do you feel?" It was so long since I had thought about my feelings I had to stop and consider awhile, in order to find out. Some Christians are all the time thinking about their feelings; and because they do not feel just right they think their joy is all gone. If we keep our faces towards Christ, and are occupied with him, we shall be lifted out of the darkness and the trouble that may have gathered around our path.

I remember being in a meeting after the War of the Great Rebellion broke out. The war had been going on for about six months. The army of the North had been defeated at Bull Run; in fact, we had nothing but defeat, and it looked as though the republic was going to pieces. So we were much cast down and discouraged. It was one of the gloomiest meetings I ever attended. Finally an old man with beautiful white hair got up to speak, and his face literally shone. "Young men," he said, "you do not talk like sons of the King. Though it is dark just here, remember it is light somewhere else." Then he went on to say that if it were dark all over the world, it was light up around the Throne.

He told us he had come from the East, where a friend had described to him how he had been up a mountain to spend the night and see the sunrise. As the party was climbing up the mountain, but before they had reached the summit, a storm came on. This friend said to the guide, "I will give this up; take me back." The guide smiled and replied, "I think we shall get above the storm soon." On they went; and it was not long before they got up to where it was as calm as any summer evening. Down in the valley a terrible storm raged; they could hear the thunder rolling, and see the lightning flash; but all was serene on the mountain top. "And so, my young friends," continued the old man, "though all is dark around you, come a little higher and the darkness will flee away." Often when I have been inclined to get discouraged, I have thought of what he said. Now if you are down in the valley amidst the thick fog and the darkness, get a little higher; get nearer to Christ, and know more of him.

You remember what the Bible says: that when Christ died on the cross, the light of the world was put out. God sent his Son to be the light of the world; but men did not love the light because it reproved them of their sins. When they were about to put out this light, what did Christ say to his disciples? "Ye shall be witnesses unto me." He has gone up yonder to intercede for us; but he wants us to shine for him down here. "Ye are the light of the world." So our work is to shine; not to blow our own trumpet so that people may look at us. What we want to do is to show forth Christ. If we have any light at all it is borrowed light. Someone said to a young Christian: "Converted! It is all moonshine!" Said he: "I thank you for the illustration; the moon borrows its light from the sun; and we borrow ours from the Sun of Righteousness." If we are Christ's, we are here to shine for him: by and by he will call us home to our reward.

I remember hearing of a blind man who sat by the wayside with a lantern near him. When he was asked what he had a lantern for, as he could not see the light, he said it was that people should not stumble over him. I believe more people stumble over the inconsistencies of professed Christians than from any other cause. What is doing more harm to the cause of Christ than all the skepticism in the world is this cold, dead formalism, this conformity to the world, this professing what we do not possess. The eyes of the world are upon us. I think it was George Fox who said that every Quaker ought to light up the country for ten miles around him. If we were all brightly shining for the Master, those about us would soon be reached, and there would be a shout of praise going to heaven.

Christ the Truth and Life

People often say: "I want to know what is the truth." "I am the truth!" says Christ. If you want to know what the truth is, get acquainted with Christ.

People also complain that they have not life. Many are trying to give themselves spiritual life. You may galvanize yourselves and put electricity into yourselves, so to speak; but the effect will not last very long. Christ alone is the author of life. If you would have real spiritual life, get to know Christ. Many try to stir up spiritual life by going to meetings. That may be well enough; but it will be of no use, unless they get into contact with the living Christ. Then their spiritual life will not be a spasmodic thing, but will be perpetual, flowing on and on, and bringing forth fruit to God.

Christ the Keeper

Christ is also our Keeper. A great many young disciples are afraid they will not hold out. "He that keepeth Israel shall neither slumber nor sleep." It is the work of Christ to keep us; and if he keeps us there will be no danger of our falling. I suppose if Queen Victoria had to take care of the Crown of England, some thief might attempt to get access to it; but it is put away in the Tower of London, and guarded night and day by soldiers. The whole English army would, if necessary, be called out to protect it.

We have no strength in ourselves. We are no match for Satan; he has had six thousand years of experience. But then we remember that the One who neither slumbers nor sleeps is our keeper. In Isaiah we read, "Fear thou not, for I am with thee;

be not dismayed, for I am thy God; I will strengthen thee; yea, I will help thee; yea, I will uphold thee with the right hand of my righteousness." In Jude also we are told that he is "able to keep us from falling." "We have an Advocate with the Father, Jesus Christ the Righteous."

Christ Our Shepherd

But Christ is even more. He is our Shepherd. It is the work of the shepherd to care for the sheep, to feed them and protect them. "I am the Good Shepherd." "My sheep hear my voice." "I lay down my life for the sheep." In that wonderful tenth chapter of John, Christ uses the personal pronoun no less than twenty-eight times in declaring what he is and what he will do. In verse 28 he says, "They shall never perish; neither shall any *man* pluck them out of my hand." But notice the word "man" is in italics. See how the verse really reads: "Neither shall *any* pluck them our of my hand"—no devil or anyone else shall be able to do it. In another place the Scripture declares, "Your life is hid with Christ in God." We are safe and secure!

Christ tells us: "My sheep hear my voice . . . and they follow me." A gentleman in the East heard of a shepherd who could call all his sheep to him by name. He went and asked if this was true. The shepherd took him to the pasture where they were, and called one of them by some name. One sheep looked up and answered the call, while the others went on feeding and paid no attention. In the same way he called about a dozen of the sheep around him. The stranger said, "How do you know one from the other? They all look perfectly alike." "Well," said the shepherd, "you see that sheep over there toes in a little; that other one has a squint; that one has a little piece of wool off; that one has a black spot; and that other has a piece out of its ear." The man knew all his sheep by their failings, for he had not a perfect one in the whole flock. I suppose our Shepherd knows us in the same way.

A shepherd was once telling a gentleman that his sheep knew his voice, and that no stranger could deceive them. The gentleman thought he would like to put the statement to the test. So he put on the shepherd's frock and turban, and took his staff and went to the flock. He disguised his voice, and tried to speak as much like the shepherd as he could; but he could not get a single sheep in the flock to follow him. He asked the shepherd if his sheep ever followed a stranger. He was obliged to admit that if a sheep got sickly it would follow anyone. So it is with a good many professed Christians; when they get sickly and weak in the faith, they will follow any teacher that comes along; but when the soul is in health, they cannot be carried away by errors and heresies. They know whether the "voice" speaks the truth or not. In the same way, when God sends a true messenger, his words will find a ready response in the Christian heart.

Christ is a tender Shepherd. You may think at times that he has not been a very tender Shepherd to you; for you are perhaps passing under the rod. It is written, "Whom the Lord loveth he chasteneth, and scourgeth every son whom he receiveth." That you are passing under the rod is no proof that Christ does not love you. A friend of mine lost all his children. No man could ever have loved his family more. But the scarlet fever took them away one by one; and so all four or five of his children, one after another, died. The poor stricken parents went over to Great Britain and the continent, wandering from one place to another. At length they found their way to Syria. One day they saw an Eastern shepherd come down to a stream, calling his flock to cross. The sheep came down to the brink, and looked at the water; but they seemed to shrink from it, and he could not get them to respond to his call. He then took a little lamb, put it under one arm; he took another lamb and put it under the other arm, and thus passed into the stream. The old sheep no longer stood looking at the water: they plunged in after the shepherd; and in a few minutes the whole flock was on the other side. He led them away to newer and fresher pastures. The bereaved father and mother, as they looked on the scene, felt that it taught them a lesson. They no longer murmured because the Great Shepherd had taken their lambs one by one into yonder world; and they began to look up and look forward to the time when they would follow the loved ones they had lost. If you have loved ones gone before, remember that your Shepherd is calling you to "set your affection on things above." Let us be faithful to him, and follow him, while we remain in this world. And if you have not taken him for your Shepherd, do so this very day.

Christ Our All in All

Christ is not only all these things that I have mentioned: he is also our Mediator, our Sanctifier, our Justifier; in fact, it would take volumes to tell what he desires to be to every individual soul. While looking through some papers I once read this wonderful description of Christ. I do not know where it originally came from; but it was so fresh to my soul that I should like to give it to you today:

> Christ is our Way; we walk in him. He is our Truth; we embrace him. He is our Life; we live in him. He is our Lord; we choose him to rule over us. He is our Master; we serve him. He is our Teacher, instructing us in the way of salvation. He is our Prophet, pointing out the future. He is our Priest, having atoned for us. He is our Advocate, ever living to make intercession for us. He is our Savior, saving to the uttermost. He is our Root; we grow from him. He is our Bread; we feed upon him. He is our Shepherd, leading us into green pastures. He is our true Vine; we abide in him. He is the Water of Life; we slake our thirst from him. He is the fairest among ten thousand: we admire him above all others. He is "the brightness of the Father's glory, and the express image of his person"; we strive to reflect his likeness. He is the upholder of all things; we rest upon him. He is our wisdom; we are guided by him. He is our Righteousness; we cast all our imperfections upon

him. He is our Sanctification; we draw all our power for holy life from him. He is our Redemption, redeeming us from all iniquity. He is our Healer, curing all our diseases. He is our Friend, relieving us in all our necessities. He is our Brother, cheering us in our difficulties.

Here is another beautiful extract from Gotthold:

For my part, my soul is like a hungry and thirsty child; and I need his love and consolation for my refreshment. I am a wandering and lost sheep; and I need him as a good and faithful shepherd. My soul is like a frightened dove pursued by the hawk; and I need his wounds for a refuge. I am a feeble vine; and I need his cross to lay hold of, and to wind myself about. I am a sinner; and I need his righteousness. I am naked and bare; and I need his holiness and innocence for a covering. I am ignorant; and I need his teaching; simple and foolish; and I need the guidance of his Holy Spirit. In no situation, and at no time, can I do without him. Do I pray? He must prompt, and intercede for me. Am I arraigned by Satan at the Divine tribunal? He must be my Advocate. Am I in affliction? He must be my Helper. Am I persecuted by the world? He must defend me, When I am forsaken, he must be my Support; when I am dying, my life: when moldering in the grave, my Resurrection. Well, then, I will rather part with all the world, and all that it contains, than with Thee, my Savior. And, God be thanked! I know that Thou, too, art neither able nor willing to do without me. Thou art rich; and I am poor. Thou hast abundance; and I am needy. Thou hast righteousness; and I sins. Thou hast wine and oil; and I wounds. Thou hast cordials and refreshments; and I hunger and thirst.

Use me then, my Savior, for whatever purpose, and in whatever way, Thou mayest require. Here is my poor heart, an empty vessel; fill it with Thy grace. Here is my sinful and troubled soul; quicken and refresh it with Thy love. Take my heart for Thine abode; my mouth to spread the glory of Thy name; my love and all my powers, for the advancement of Thy believing people; and never suffer the steadfastness and confidence of my faith to abate—that so at all times I may be enabled from the heart to say, "Jesus needs me, and I him; and so we suit each other."

Courage and Enthusiasm

JOSHUA 1

Only be thou strong and very courageous, that thou mayest observe to do according to all the law, which Moses my servant commanded thee: turn not from it to the right hand or to the left, that thou mayest prosper whithersoever thou goest.

Courage

I shall take for my subject tonight only two words, courage and enthusiasm—necessary qualifications for successful work in the Lord's service. In the first chapter of Joshua, God tells Joshua four different times to be of good courage, for if he is of good courage, no man will be able to stand before him all the days of his life. And we read that in the evening of his life, he was successful and no man was able to stand before him all his days. God fulfilled his promise. God kept his word. But see how careful

God is to instruct him on this one point. Four times in one chapter he says to him, "Be of good courage, and then you shall prosper, then you shall have good success."

I have yet to find that God ever uses a man that is all the time looking on the dark side, and is all the time talking about the obstacles and looking at them, and is discouraged and cast down. It is not these Christians that go around with their head down like a bulrush, looking at the obstacles and talking about the darkness all the time, that God uses. They kill everything they touch. There is no life in them. Now if we are going to succeed we have got to be of good courage, and the moment we get our eyes on God and remember who he is, and that he has all power in heaven and earth, that it is God that commands us to work in his vineyard, then it is that we will have courage given us.

If you will take your Bibles and look carefully through them, you will see the men that have left their mark behind them; the men that have been successful in winning souls to Christ have all been men of that stamp. Moses, for example, after he had been among the Egyptians forty years, thought the time had come for him to commence his work of delivering the captives. He went out, and the first thing we hear is that he was looking this way and that way to see if somebody called him. He was not fit for God's work. God had to take him on the back side of the desert for forty years, and then God was ready to send him, and Moses then looked but one way. And he sent him down to Egypt. He had boldness now, and he went before the king of Egypt, and he had courage and God could use him. But it took him forty years to learn that he must have courage and boldness to be a fit vessel for the Master's use.

Elijah, on Mount Carmel, was full of boldness. How the Lord used him! How the Lord stood by him! How the Lord blessed him! But when he got his eyes off the way, and Jezebel sent a message to him that she would have his life, he got afraid. He was not afraid of Ahab. He was not afraid of the whole nation. He stood on Mount Carmel alone. But what came over him when he got Jezebel's message, I do not know, unless it was that he got his eyes off the Lord. One woman's message got him frightened.

That, I think, is the trouble with a good many of God's people. We get frightened, and are afraid to speak to men about their souls. We lack moral courage, and if we hear the voice of God speaking to us and saying, "Run and speak to that young man," we will go to him meaning to do it, but will only talk to him about everything else, and not about his soul. When we begin to invite them to Christ is when the work of God begins, and it won't begin until we have the courage given us and are ready to go and speak with people about their souls. We read that when the apostles were brought before the council they perceived their boldness, and it made an impression on the council. The Lord could use them then, because they were fearless and bold. Look at Peter on Pentecost. Yet only a little while before he had got out of communion, and one little maid had scared him nearly out of his life, so that he swore he didn't know Christ. Ah! He had his eyes off the Master, and the moment we get our eyes off Christ we get disheartened, and then God cannot use us.

I remember a few years ago I got discouraged and could not see much fruit in my work. One morning, as I was in my study, cast down, one of my Sabbath school teachers came in and wanted to know what I was discouraged about, and I told him it was because I could see no result from my work. Speaking about Noah he said: "By the way, did you ever study the character of Noah?" I felt that I knew all about that, and told him that I was familiar with it. He said, "Now, if you never studied that carefully, you ought to do it, for I cannot tell you what a blessing it has been to me." When he went out I took down my Bible and commenced to read about Noah, and the thought came stealing over me, "Here is a man that toiled and worked a hundred years and didn't get discouraged; or if he did, the Holy Ghost didn't put it on record." Suddenly, the clouds lifted, and I got up and said, if the Lord wants me to work without any fruit I will work on. I went down to the noon prayer-meeting, and when I saw the people coming to pray I said to myself, "Noah worked a hundred years, and he never saw a prayer-meeting outside of his own family." Pretty soon a man got up across the aisle from where I was sitting, and said he had come from a little town where a hundred united with the Church of God the year before. And I thought to myself, "What if Noah had heard that! He preached so many, many years and didn't get a convert, yet he was not discouraged." Then a man got up right behind me, and he trembled as he said, "I am lost. I want you to pray for my soul." And I said, "What if Noah had heard that! He worked a hundred and twenty years, and never had a man come to him and said that; and yet he didn't get discouraged." And I made up my mind then, that, God helping me, I would never get discouraged. I would do the best I could, and leave the results with God.

And so let me say to the Christians of New York, that we must expect good results, and never get discouraged. But if we don't get good results, let us not look on the dark side, but keep on praying, and in the fullness of time the blessing of God will come. What we want is to have the Christians come out and take their stand. I find a great many professed Christians ashamed to acknowledge that they have been quickened. Some have said they did not like the idea of asking Christians to rise, as I did last evening; that it was putting them in a false position. Now, if we are going to be successful, we have got to take our stand for God, and let the world and everyone know we are on the Lord's side.

I have great respect for the woman that started out during the war with a poker. She heard the enemy was coming and went to resist them. When someone asked her what she could do with the poker, she said she would at least let them know what side she was on. And that is what we want, and the time is coming when the line must be drawn in this city, and those on Christ's side must take their stand. The moment we come out boldly and acknowledge Christ, then it is that men will begin to inquire what they must do to be saved.

Enthusiasm

Then there is a class of people that is not warm enough. I don't think a little enthusiasm would hurt the Church at the present time. I think we need it. I know the world will cry out against it. Business men will cry out against religious enthusiasm. Let railroad stocks go up fifteen or twenty percent, and see what a revival would break out in business. Let the stock market advance suddenly, and see what enthusiasm would follow. Let there be a sudden change in business, and see if there isn't a good deal of enthusiasm on the street. We can have enthusiasm in business, we can have enthusiasm in politics, and no one complains of that. A man can have enthusiasm in everything else, but the moment that a little fire gets into the church they raise the cry, "Ah, enthusiasm—false excitement—I am afraid of it."

I do not want false excitement, but I do think we want a little fire, a little holy enthusiasm. But some will raise the cry, "Zeal without knowledge." Yet, I would rather have zeal without knowledge than knowledge without zeal, and it won't hurt us to have a little more of this enthusiasm and zeal in the Lord's work.

I saw more zeal when I was in Princeton last Sunday than I have in many a year. I was talking to the students there about their souls, and after I had been talking for some time, quite a group of young men gathered around me, and the moment that one of them made a surrender and said, "I will accept Christ," it seems as if there were twenty-five hands stretched out to shake his. That is what we want—men that will rejoice to hear news of the conversion of other men. Although I don't admire his ideas, I do admire the enthusiasm of that man Garibaldi. It is reported that when he marched toward Rome in 1867, they took him up and threw him into prison, and he sat right down and wrote to his comrades: "If fifty Garibaldis are thrown into prison let Rome be free." That is the spirit. Who is Garibaldi? He is nothing. "If fifty Garibaldis are thrown into prison let Rome be free." That is what we want in the cause of Christ. We have got to work, and not be loitering at our ease.

But the question of dignity comes up. We have got to lay all that aside to become helpers. What difference does it make whether we are "hewers of wood" or "carriers of water" while the Temple of God is being erected?

Yes, let us have an enthusiasm in the Church of God. If we had it in a few of the churches in New York, I believe it would be like a resurrection. The people would say, "What has come over this man? He's not the same man he was two months ago." We want to have them say: "The Son of God is dearer to us than our money. The Son of God is dearer to us than our families. The Son of God is dearer to us than our position in society." Let us do anything, that the work of God may go on. When we get there, God will bless us. As it says in the Bible: "One shall chase a thousand." We have not got many of that kind in our churches today. I wish we had more of them. The Bible says: "Two shall put ten thousand to flight." Now, if a few should lay hold of God in this way, see what a great army will rise in this city! We cannot be lukewarm; we have got to be on fire with the cause of Christ. We have got to have more of this enthusiasm that will carry us into the Lord's work. If there is going to be a great revival in New York, it's not going to be in this hall. It has got to be done by one and another going around and talking to their neighbors. There isn't a skeptic, there isn't a drunkard, but what can be reclaimed if we come with desire in our hearts. There is a story from the ninth century, I believe, of a young man that came up with a little handful of men to attack a king who had a great army of three thousand men. The young man had only five hundred, and the king sent a messenger to the young man, saying that he need not fear to surrender, for he would be treated mercifully. The young man called up one of his soldiers and said: "Take this dagger and drive it to your heart"; and the soldier took the dagger and drove it to his heart. And calling up another, he said to him, "Leap into yonder chasm," and the man leaped into the chasm. The young man then said to the messenger: "Go back and tell your king I have got five hundred men like these. We will die, but we will never surrender. And tell your king another thing, that I will have him chained with my dog inside half an hour." And when the king heard that, he did not dare to meet them, and his army fled before them like chaff before the wind. And within twenty-four hours he had that king chained with his dog.

This is the kind of zeal we want. "We will die but we will never surrender." We will work until Jesus comes, and then we will rise with him. Oh, if men are willing to die for patriotism, why can they not have the same zeal for Christ? All that Abraham Lincoln had to do was to call for volunteers, and how speedily they came. When he called for six hundred thousand, how quickly they sprang up all over the nation. Are not souls worth more than this republic? Are not souls worth more than this government? Don't we want six hundred thousand men? If even six hundred men should come forward whose hearts were right red-hot for the Son of God, we would be able to see what mighty results would follow. "One man shall chase a thousand, and two shall put ten thousand to flight." In time of war, the generals that were all the time on the defensive never succeeded. The generals that were successful were the generals that were on the offensive. Some of our churches think they are doing remarkably well if they hold their membership, and they think if they have thirty or forty conversions in that church during the year, they are doing a remarkable work. They think it is enough to supply the places of those who have died and those who have wandered away during the past. It seems to me we ought to bring thousands and thousands to Christ.

I say the time has come for us to have a war on the offensive side. There may be barriers in our path, but God can remove them. There may be a mountain in our way, but God can take us over the mountain. There may be difficulties in the way, but he can overcome them. Our God is above them all, and if the Church of God is ready to advance, all obstacles will be removed. No man ever sent by God ever failed, but self must be lost sight of. We must be willing to lay down our lives for the cause of Christ.

When I was going to Europe in 1867, my friend Mr. Stuart, of Philadelphia, said: "Be sure to be at the General Assembly in Edinburgh, in June. I was there last year," said he, "and it did me a world of good." He said that a returned missionary from India was invited to speak to the General Assembly, on the wants of India. This old missionary, after a brief address, told the pastors who were present, to go home and stir up their churches and send young men to India to preach the gospel. He spoke with such earnestness, that after a while he fainted, and they carried him from the hall. When he recovered he asked where he was, and they told him the circumstances under which he had been brought there. "Yes," he said, "I was making a plea for India, and I didn't quite finish my speech, did I?" After being told that he did not, he said, "Well, take me back and let me finish it." But they said, "No, you will die in the attempt." "Well," said he, "I will die if I don't," and the old man asked again that they would allow him to finish his plea. When he was taken back the whole congregation stood as one man, and as they brought him on the platform, with a trembling voice he said: "Fathers and mothers of Scotland, is it true that you will not let your sons go to India? I spent twenty-five years of my life there. I lost my health, and I have come back with sickness and shattered health. If it is true that we have no strong grandsons to go to India, I will pack up what I have and be off tomorrow, and I will let those heathens know that if I cannot live for them I will die for them."

The world would say that that old man was enthusiastic. Well, that is just what we want. No doubt that is what they said of the Son of God when he was down here. Oh, that God may baptize us tonight with the spirit of enthusiasm! That he may anoint us tonight with the Holy Ghost! Let me say to some of you men—I see some gray locks here, who I have no doubt are saying, "I wish I was young again; I would like to help in this work. I would like to work for the Lord." When we went to London there was an eighty-five-year-old woman, who came to the meetings and said she wanted a hand in that work. She was appointed to a district, and called on all classes of people. She went to places where younger folk would probably have been put out, telling the people of Christ. There were none that could resist her. When she offered to pray for people, they all received her kindly. That is enthusiasm. That is what we want in New York. If you cannot give a day to this work, give an hour, or if not an hour, give five minutes. If you have not strength to do anything personally, you can pray for this work. Now, it is a good deal better to do that than it is to stand off and criticize. Some will say, "O, I heard my grandfather say how such things should be done. This is not managed right to be successful." And they stand off and criticize and find fault, and we will never succeed as long as they do this. All of us should work and ask for God's guidance as we do.

Once, when a great fire broke out in the middle of the night, way up there in the fifth story of the building, they spotted a little child, crying for help. Up went a ladder, and soon a fireman was seen ascending to the spot. As he neared the second story the flames burst in fury from the windows, and the multitude almost despaired of the rescue of the child. The brave man faltered, and a comrade at the bottom cried out, "Cheer!" and cheer upon cheer arose from the crowd. Up the ladder he went and saved the child, because they cheered him. If you cannot go into the heat of the battle yourself, if you cannot go into the harvest field and work day after day, you can cheer those that are working for the Master. Many old people in their old days get crusty and sour, and they discourage everyone they meet by their fault finding. That is not what we want. If we make a mistake, come and tell us of it, and we will thank you. You don't know how much you may do by just speaking kindly to those that are willing to work.

I remember when I was a boy I went several miles from home with an older brother. That seemed to me the longest visit of my life. It seemed that I was then further away from home than I had ever been before, or have ever been since. While we were walking down the street we saw an old man coming toward us, and my brother said, "There is a man that will give you a cent. He gives every new boy that comes into this town a cent." That was my first visit to the town, and when the old man got opposite to us he looked around, and my brother—not wishing me to lose the cent—reminded the old man that I was a new boy in the town. The old man, taking off my hat, placed his trembling hand on my head, and told me I had a Father in heaven. It was a kind, simple act, but I feel the pressure of the old man's hand upon my head today.

We can all do something in this work of saving souls. That is what we have come to this city for. There is not a mother, a father, nor wife, there is not a young man in all the city, but what ought to be in sympathy with this work. We have come here to try to save souls. I never heard of one that was brought to Christ who was injured by coming. Oh, let us pray for the Spirit of God; let us pray that this spirit of criticism and of fault finding may be all laid aside, and that we may be of one spirit as they were on the day of Pentecost.

To Every Man His Work

MARK 13:34

For the Son of Man is as a man taking a far journey, who left his house, and gave authority to his servants, and to every man his work, and commanded the porter to watch.

I want to call your attention to a verse you will find in the thirteenth chapter of Mark, part of the thirty-fourth verse—"to every man his work." "For the Son of Man is as a man taking a far journey, who left his house and gave authority to his servants, and to every man his work, and commanded the porter to watch." Now, that verse doesn't read, "to every man some work," or "to every man a work," but "to every man his work." And I believe if the truth was known that every man and woman in this assembly has a work laid out for them to do; that every man's life is a plan of the Almighty, and way back in the councils of eternity, God laid out a work for each one of us.

There is no man living that can do the work that God has got for me to do. No one can do it but myself. And if the work isn't done, we will each have to answer for it when we stand before God's bar. For the Bible says: "Every man shall be brought unto judgment, and everyone shall give an account of the deeds done in the body." And it seems to me that every one of us ought to take this question home tonight: "Am I doing the work that God has for me to do?" God has got a work for every one of us to do.

In the parable told by our Lord, the man who had two talents had the same reward as the man who had five talents. He heard the same words as the man who had five talents. "Well done, thou good and faithful servant, enter thou into the joy of thy Lord." To those who take good care of the talents that God has loaned them, even more are given. But if we take the talent that God has given us and lay it away carefully in a napkin and bury it away, God will take even that talent from us. God doesn't expect a man that has got one talent to do the work of a man that has got ten. All a man has got to answer for is that which God has given him. If we were all of us doing the work that God has got for us to do, don't you see how the work of the Lord would advance? I believe what John Wesley used to say: "All at it, and always at it." That is what the Church needs to say.

But some will say, "I don't believe in these revivals; they're only temporary, they only last a few minutes." Yes, if I thought it was only to last a few minutes, I would also say "Amen." My prayer has been for years that God will let me die when the spirit of revival dies out in my heart, and I don't want to live any longer if I can't be used to some purpose. What are we all down in this world of sickness and sorrow for unless it is to work for the Son of God, and improve the talents he has given us. But some are not satisfied with the talents they have, but are always wishing for someone else's talent. Now, that is all wrong. It is contrary to the Spirit of Christ. Instead of wishing for someone else's talent, let us make the best use of the talents God has given us. Now, there isn't a father or a mother here but would think it a great misfortune if their children did not grow for the next ten or fifteen years. That little boy there, if he shouldn't grow any for ten or fifteen years, his mother would say, "It is a great calamity." Yet, I know some men of my acquaintance who make the same prayers they made fifteen or twenty years ago. They are like a horse in a tread-mill—it is always the same old story of their experiences when they were converted, and going round and round.

Let us do all the business we can. If we can't be a lighthouse, let us be a tallow candle. There used to be a period when the people came up to meeting bringing their candles with them. The first one perhaps wouldn't make a great illumination, but when two or three got there there would be more light. If the people of this city should do that now, if each one should come here with our candle, don't you think there would be a little light? Let all the gas be put out in this hall and one solitary candle would give a good deal of light here. If we can't be a lighthouse let us be a tallow candle. Someone said, "I can't be anything more than a farthing rushlight." Well, if you can't be more be that, that is well enough. Be all you can.

What makes the Dead Sea dead? Because it is all the time receiving, never giving out anything. Why is it that many Christians are cold? Because they are all the time receiving, never giving out anything. You go every Sunday and hear good sermons, and think that is enough. You are all the time receiving these grand truths but never giving them out. When you hear it, go and scatter the sacred truth abroad. Instead of having one minister to preach to a thousand people, the thousand ought to take the sermon and spread it till it reaches those that never go to church or chapel. Instead of having a few, we ought to have thousands using the precious talents that God has given them.

Now, Andrew got the reputation of bringing people to Christ. He went about it in the right way; he began right. I imagine that when Christ wanted mighty deeds done, he went out and hunted up Andrew. Andrew inquired of the people, "Have you seen anything of Peter?" And when he found him he brought him to Christ. Little did Andrew know of the importance of the day when he brought Peter to Christ. Little did he think that on that day he did the greatest act of his life. What joy must have filled his heart when he saw three thousand brought under the influence of the Spirit by that holy man. Oh, you cannot tell what results will follow if you just improve the talent God has given you by bringing one Simon Peter to Christ. Then we read that when the Greeks came and wanted to see Jesus, Andrew met them and brought them all to Christ. Andrew had a reputation of bringing sinners to God. That is a good reputation. I would rather have that reputation than any other. Oh, the joy there is in bringing people to Christ! This is what we all can do if we will. If God has not given us but half a talent, let us make good use of that.

When Jesus told the people to take their seats by fifties, he told Philip to get food for them. "What," said Philip, "feed them with this little loaf? Why, there is not more than enough for the first man." "Yes, go and feed them with that," our Lord said. Philip thought that was a very small amount for such a multitude of hungry men. He broke off a piece for the first man, and didn't miss it; a piece for the second man, and didn't miss it; a piece for the third man, and didn't miss it. He was making good use of the loaf, and God kept increasing it. That is what the Lord wants to do with us. He will give us just as many talents as we can take care of.

There are many of us that are willing to do great things for the Lord, but few of us willing to do little things. The mighty sermon on regeneration was preached to one man. There are many who are willing to preach to thousands, but are not willing to take their seat beside one soul, and lead that soul to the blessed Jesus. We must get down to personal effort—this bringing one by one to the Son of God.

We can find no better example of this than in the life of Christ himself. Look at that wonderful sermon that he preached to that lone woman at the well of Samaria. He was tired and weary, but he had time and the heart to preach to her. This is but one of many instances in the life of the Master from which we may learn a precious lesson. If the Son of God had time to preach to one soul, cannot every one of us go and do the same?

If people, instead of merely coming to these meetings, folding up their arms and enjoying themselves, without personal effort, would wake up to the fact that they have a work to do, what a wonderful work could be done! It is not enough simply to come to these meetings: we need ten thousand workers in New York City. We need ten thousand men and women that are willing to say, "Lord, here am I, use me." Ten thousand of such people would revolutionize this city. Look at the work of the mighty Wesley. The world never saw a hundred such men living at the same time. The trouble is, we are afraid to speak to men about their souls. Let us ask God to give us grace to overcome this man-fearing spirit. There is a wife, but she dare not speak to her husband about his soul. There is a father that dare not speak to a son about his soul. What we want to do is to speak to our neighbors about these things. We call it a little work, but let me say to you it is a great deal. If we would do this we might turn ten thousand to the Son of God.

I remember hearing of a person that was always trying to do some great thing for the Lord, and because he could not do a great thing, he never did anything. There are a great many who would be willing to do great things if they could come up and have their names heralded through the press. I remember hearing of a man's dream, in which he imagined that when he died he was taken by the angels to a beautiful temple. After admiring it for a time, he discovered that one stone was missing. All finished but just one little stone; that was left out. He said to the angel, "What is this stone left out for?" The angel replied, "That was left out for you, but you wanted to do great things, and so there was no room left for you." He was startled, and awoke, and resolved that he would become a worker for God, and that man always worked faithfully after that.

Now, my friends, we must not expect to do great things. We must take anything that comes to us. We must let the Lord use us as he sees fit. I remember once, while preaching at a meeting, of noticing in the congregation a lady who had a class in a mission school. I knew that it was the time for them to meet, and I wondered what she was there for. When I got home, I said, "How did you happen to be at the meeting this afternoon? What did you do with all those little lambs? Haven't you a class that meets today?" "Yes," she said, "but I only have five little boys, and I didn't think it would matter if I didn't teach them today." "Have you five little boys?" "Yes." "How do you know but among those little boys there may be a Knox, there may be a Wesley, or a Whitefield, or a Bunyan? There may be a man there who will go out and revolutionize the world." My friends, in that little boy with his tattered clothes and uncombed hair, there may be a Martin Luther, if you could but lead him to Christ. If you have five little children come to you, thank God for that, and start with your work.

I heard, some time ago, of a young lady that went out to a boarding school. Her parents were very wealthy, and sent her to the best school they could find. They were very anxious that their daughter should shine in the highest circle of society, that she should become refined and educated. Among her associates at school was a lady who loved and worked for Christ. By constant labor she won this young girl's heart, and pleaded with her to become a Christian. She succeeded, and the young lady became a worker in the vineyard of the Lord. She taught her the luxury of working for Christ. She labored with her schoolmates, and God used her in winning quite a number of young ladies in that school to Christ. I have known a great many ministers who wanted to know how they could keep their congregation out of the world. Give them so much to do that they won't have time to attend to cherished worldly influences.

This young lady of whom I was speaking came home, and her father and mother wanted her to shine in fashionable society. No, she said, she had got something better than that. She went to the Sabbath school superintendent, and said to him, "Can you give me a class in the Sunday school?" He was surprised that this young lady should want that. He told her that he had no class that he could give her then. She went away with a resolve to do what she could outside of the school. One day, as she was walking up the street, she saw a little boy running out of a shoemaker's shop, and behind him was the old shoemaker, chasing him, with a wooden last in his hand. He had not run far until the wooden shoe form was thrown at him, and he was struck in the back. The boy stopped and began to cry. The Spirit of the Lord touched that young lady's heart, and she went to where he was. She stepped up to him and asked him if he was hurt. He told her it was none of her business. She went to work then to win that boy's confidence. She asked him if he went to school. He said, "No." "Well, why don't you go to school?" "Don't want to." She asked him if he would not like to go to Sunday school. "If you will come," she said, "I will tell you beautiful stories, and read nice books." She coaxed and pleaded with him, and at last said that if he would consent to go she would meet him on the corner of the street which they should agree upon. He at last consented, and the next Sunday, true to his promise, he waited for her at the place designated. She took him by the hand and led him into the Sabbath school. "Can you give me a place to teach this little boy?" she asked of the superintendent. He looked at the boy, but they didn't have any ones who looked like that in the school.

A place was found, however, and she sat down in the corner with the boy and tried to win that soul for Christ. Many would look upon her efforts with contempt, but she had got something to do for the Master. The little boy had never heard anybody sing so sweetly before. When he went home he was asked where he had been. "I've been among the angels," he told his mother. He said he had been to the Protestant Sabbath school; but his father and mother told him he must not go there any more or he would get a flogging. The next Sunday he went, and when he came home he got the promised flogging. He went the second time and got a flogging, and also a third time with the same result. At last he said to his father, "I wish you would flog me before I go, and then I won't have to think of it when I am there." The father said, "If you go to that Sabbath school again I will kill you."

It was the father's custom to send his son out on the street to sell articles to the passers-by, and he told the boy that he might have the profits of what he sold on Saturday. The little fellow hastened to the young lady's house and said to her, "Father said that he would give me every Saturday to myself, and if you will just teach me then, I will come to your house every Saturday afternoon." I wonder how many young ladies there are that would give up their Saturday afternoons just to teach one boy the way into the kingdom of God? Every Saturday afternoon that little boy was there at her house, and she tried to tell him the way to Christ. She labored with him, and at last the light of God's Spirit broke upon his heart.

One day while he was selling his wares at the railroad station, a train of cars approached unnoticed, and passed over both his legs. A physician was summoned, and the first thing after he arrived, the little sufferer looked up into his face, and said, "Doctor, will I live to get home?" "No," said the doctor, "you are dying." "Will you tell my mother and father that I died a Christian?" They bore home the boy's corpse, and with it the last message that he died a Christian. Oh, what a noble work was that young lady's in saving that little wanderer! How precious the remembrance to her! When she goes to heaven she will not be a stranger there. He will take her by the hand and lead her to the throne of Christ. She did the work cheerfully. Oh, may God teach us what our work is, that we may do it for his glory.

It is the greatest pleasure of living to win souls to Christ, and it is a pleasure that angels can't enjoy. It is sometimes a wonder to me that God doesn't take the work out of the church and give it to the angels. If the redeemed saints could come by the bar, I sometimes think they would rejoice in coming back here to have the privilege of leading one more soul to Christ. Isn't it high time that the church got awake from its midnight slumber? It is time the work was commenced, and when the Spirit of God revives it, shan't we go and do it? Are there not five thousand Christians in this hall, and is there not someone among them that can lead a soul to Christ within the next week? If we work, what a great army can be brought in, if we are only faithful! I want to say to the Christians here that there is one rule I have followed that has helped me wonderfully. I made it a rule that I wouldn't let a day pass without speaking to someone about their soul's salvation, and if they didn't hear the gospel from the lips of others, there will be 365 in a year that shall hear the gospel from my lips. There are five thousand Christians here tonight; can't they say, "We won't let a day pass without speaking a word to someone about the cause of Christ"?

At a place where we were holding meetings, in the gasworks, there was a man who came to our very first meeting. He was very much interested, and said, "I will try and see if I can't lead some of the men in my shop to Christ." He began to talk with them. There were one hundred seventy-five men on the nightwatch, and when I left they said twenty-five of them had been converted; and every night, at midnight—that is the hour they have what might be called their midnight dinner—they have a prayer-meeting. When you and I sleep tonight all these young converts speak and pray, and it looks now as if every man in the gas-works is going to be brought to Christ.

When we were in Belfast, there was a man who heard about leading souls to Christ. He began by talking to his wife, and to his servant, and to his children; and just as we were leaving Belfast they were very much interested, but not converted. He came down to Dublin—broke up his home, left his business, and came to Dublin. One night he came to me joyously and said: "My wife has been converted." A little while after, he came and said, "My younger son has been converted"; and a little while after, he said, "My oldest son has been converted."

And now the whole family is in the ark. And he came over to Manchester, and he came up to London; and now perhaps in all Belfast there is not one that works harder than that whole family. Look at this man's success. He found his work was right there in his own household; and if the fathers, and mothers, and sisters, and wives, and brothers will try to bring the members of their families to Christ, and cry, "O God, teach me what my work is"—the Spirit of God will surely tell them what their work is, and then if they are ready to go and do it, there will be thousands converted in this city in a few days. Oh, may the Spirit of the Lord come upon us tonight, and may every one of us be taught by the Holy Ghost what our work is, and may we be ready to do it.

Love and Sympathy 

1 CORINTHIANS 13

Though I speak with the tongues of men and of angels, and have not charity, I am become as sounding brass, or a tinkling cymbal. . . . And though I bestow all my goods to feed the poor, and though I give my body to be burned, and have not charity, it profiteth me nothing.

There are two qualifications which we need in order to be successful fishers of men, in order to be successful in winning souls to Christ: namely, love and sympathy. I want to call your attention to the thirteenth chapter of 1 Corinthians, where it says: "If I speak with the tongues of men and of angels and have not charity, I am become as sounding brass or a tinkling cymbal"; and "if we even give our bodies to be burned and yet if we haven't real love in our hearts, our work will go for naught." In Titus chapter two we read: "But speak thou the things which become sound doctrine; that the aged men may be sober, grave, temperate, sound in faith, in charity and in patience."

If love does not prompt all our work, it will be for naught. If a man in the church is not sound in his faith, we draw our ecclesiastical sword and cut his head right off; but if he is not sound in love, we do nothing. The great want in our churches today is the want of love in them. If we had more love we would do better, for love begets love, and then, too, hate begets hate. You often hear a man say that "such and such is the meanest man in town." Now the other man may have had no ill-feeling towards the speaker, but if he hears of the remark he begins to think badly of the one who abused him, and soon learns to hate him. Now, if a man should hear that another man loves him and has spoken well of him, his love will grow too. Christ tells us all: "By this shall all men know that you are Christians because you have love one for another." This love will be the badge of the Christian, like the badges the ushers wear here.

Without love we are not really converted. When we are truly converted we love all things and all men better than ever before. The morning I was converted, I went out and I fell in love with the bright sun shining over the earth; I never loved the sun before. And when I heard the birds singing their sweet songs, I fell in love with the birds, like the Scottish lassie who stood on the hills of her native land, breathing the sweet air, and when asked why she did it, said: "I love the Scottish air." If the church was filled with love, it could do so much more.

Duty

I am tired of the word "duty"; tired of hearing "duty, duty, duty." Men go to church because it is their duty. They go to prayer meeting because it is their duty. You can never reach a man's heart if you talk to him because it is your duty. Suppose I told my wife I loved her because it was my duty—what would she say? Once every year I go up to Connecticut to visit my aged mother. Suppose, when I go next time, I tell her that I knew she was old and that she was living on borrowed time; that I knew she had always done a great deal for me, and that I came to see her every year because it was my duty. Don't you think she would say, "Well, then, my son, you needn't take the trouble to come again"?

Let us strike for a higher plane. God loved the world when it was full of sinners and those who broke his law. If he did so, can't we do it, and love our fellow men? If the Savior could die for the world, can't we work for it? The churches would soon be filled if outsiders could find that people in them loved them when they came, if the elders and deacons were glad to see them and were ready to take them by the hand and welcome them. Such things would draw sinners. Actions like these speak louder than words.

More Than Spoken Love

We do not want to talk of love and not show it in our deeds; we want something more than spoken love. If our heart goes out towards them and we love them, they will be drawn towards us and we will win them to Christ. We must win them to us first and then we can win them to Christ. The last time I heard Dr. Arnold speak—he died soon afterward—he used a homely illustration. Said he, "Those of you who were brought up on a farm will understand it. When you have to wean a calf you have to teach it how to drink. You take a bucket of milk and then you put your fingers in the calf's mouth, and when he has got a good hold you pull his nose right down into the milk. Then you slip your fingers out, and then the calf is drinking before he knows anything about it." "So," said he, "you must get the people to love you, and then turn them over to Christ." We must be more lovely ourselves, and show the people that we love them.

In our city a few years ago there was a little boy who went to one of the mission Sunday schools. His father moved to another part of the city about five miles away, and every Sunday that boy came past thirty or forty Sunday schools to the one he attended. And one Sunday a lady who was out collecting scholars for a Sunday school met him and asked him why he went so far, past so many schools. "There are plenty of others," said she, "just as good." He said, "They may be as good, but they are not so good for me." "Why not?" she asked. "Because they love a fellow over there," he answered. Ah! love won him. "Because they love a fellow over there!" How easy it is to reach people through love! Sunday school teachers should win the affections of their scholars if they wish to lead them to Christ. Those who are successful in winning the affections of men are successful in leading them to Christ.

Won by a Smile

In London, in 1872, one Sunday morning a minister said to me, "I want you to notice that family there in one of the front seats, and when we go home I want to tell you their story." When we got home I asked him for the story, and he said, "That family was won by a smile." "Why," said I, "How's that?" "Well," said he, "as I was walking down a street one day I saw a child at a window; she smiled, and I smiled, and we bowed. So it was the second time; I bowed, she bowed. It was not long before there was another child, and I had got in a habit of looking and bowing, and pretty soon the group grew, and at last, as I went by, a lady was with them. I didn't know what to do. I didn't want to bow to her, but I knew the children expected it, and so I bowed to them all. And the mother saw I was a minister, because I carried a Bible every Sunday morning. So the children followed me the next Sunday and found I was a minister. And they thought I was the greatest preacher, and their parents must hear me. A minister who is kind to a child and gives him a pat on the head, why the children will think he is the greatest preacher in the world. Kindness goes a great way. And to make a long story short, the father and mother and five children were converted, and they are going to join our church next Sunday."

Won to Christ by a smile! We must get the wrinkles out of our brows, and we must have smiling faces. The world is after the best thing, and we must show them that we have got something better than infidelity. We must convince them of this, or those that live away from Christ will stumble over us into the last world. Men are after the best thing everywhere, and we must show the world that we have got the best thing before we win the world. If a man is after a horse, he wants to get the best horse he can for the money. If a lady goes shopping, she wants to get the best ribbon she can for the money. If a man wants a coat, he wants to get the best coat he can for the money. This is the desire the world around. If we show men that religion is better than anything else, we shall win the world, but we cannot do it if we are cold and lukewarm, and under the lashings of conscience all the time.

We won't win the world to Christ if we are cold and lukewarm; but if the love of God beats in warm pulsations in our hearts, and we show them we are full of love and sympathy for them, how easy it will be to win souls to Christ! I like to see in a Christian's face the light that comes down from the celestial hills of glory. To love those that abuse them; that is what the Master did; and if we have his Spirit, we will certainly love those that don't love us. I don't think there is a man in New York whose heart is so hard but that love will break it.

A friend of mine who had a large Sabbath school, had a theory never to turn a boy out of Sabbath school on account of bad conduct. "I considered," said he, "that those boys who behaved badly in Sunday school had not had the advantages of a good bringing up, and for that very reason ought not to be turned out. I found out," said he, "that it was one thing to have a theory and another thing to put it in practice." For he had a boy come into his Sunday school that nearly upset all his practice. He put him under one teacher, and nothing could be done with him; he put him under another teacher, and nothing could be done with him; he put him under another teacher, and nothing could be done with him, and he made up his mind to expel him from the school, and do it publicly, and let all the school know that the boy was expelled.

But there came a lady teacher to him, who said, "I wish you would let me have that boy." "But," said he, "he is such a bad boy; he uses such vulgar language. All those men can't do anything with him, and I think, I am sure you can't." The lady said, "I am not doing much for Christ, and it may be that I can win him." But she was a lady of refined society, and he thought, "Surely, she won't be willing to have patience with that boy." He gave her the boy, and, he said, for a few Sundays he behaved very well, but one Sunday he behaved badly, and she corrected him, and he up and spat in her face. She quietly took her handkerchief and wiped her face. I don't know what his name was, but we will call him Johnny. "Johnny," she said, "I wish you would go home with me. I want to talk with you." "Well, I won't," he said, "I won't be seen on the street with you, and what's more, I won't ever come to this Sunday school any more." "Well," she said, "if you won't walk home with me, let me walk home with you." No, he said he wouldn't be seen on the street with her, and he was not coming to that dirty old Sunday school any more. She knew if she was going to reach that boy, she must do it then, and she thought she would try. She thought she would just bear on that curiosity chord. Sometimes, when you can't reach people in any other way, you can do it by exciting their curiosity. She said to him, "If you will come to my house, next Tuesday morning, I shan't be there; but if you will go there and ring the front door bell, and tell the servant there is a little bundle on the bureau for you, she will give it to you." The little fellow said he wouldn't come. She thought he might change his mind. He thought it over, and he thought he would just like to know what there was in that bundle. And he went up to the house Tuesday morning, and the bundle was handed to him; and there was a little vest in it, and a little necktie that she had made with her own hands, and a kind note stating that ever since he had been in her class she had been praying for him every morning and every evening, and she told him how she loved him and cared for him. The next morning he was there, bright and early, before she was up. The servant came up and told her that that boy was in the drawing room, and wanted to see her. She went down, and found the little fellow sitting on the sofa, weeping. She spoke to him kindly, and said, "What is the trouble?" And he says, "O teacher, I have had no peace since I got that note from you." And she got down and prayed with him. "And," said the superintendent, "there is not a better boy in the school." Love conquered him.

Love Conquers All

The greatest infidel can be reached by love. The greatest drunkard can be reached by love. Infidelity doesn't know anything about love. The religion of Jesus Christ is a religion of love. If we would be successful workers in his vineyard it is the love of Christ that must bind us together. A few years ago I was in a town down in our state, the guest of a family that had a little boy about thirteen years old, who did not bear the family name, yet was treated like the rest. Every night, when he retired, the lady of the house kissed him and treated him in every respect like all the other children. I think he was the finest-looking boy I have ever seen. I said to her, "I don't understand it." She said, "I want to tell you about that boy. That boy is the son of a missionary. His father and mother were missionaries in India, but they found they had got to bring their children back to this country to educate them. So they gave up their mission field and came back to educate their children and to find some missionary work to do in this country. But they were not prospered here as they had been in India, and the father said, 'I will go back to India'; and the mother said, 'If God has called you to go I am sure it will be my duty to go, and my privilege to go, and I will go with you.' The father said, 'You have never been separated from the children, and it will be hard for you to be separated from them; perhaps you had better stay and take care of them.' But after prayer they decided to leave their children to be educated, and they left for India." This lady heard of it and sent a letter to the parents, in which she stated if they left one child at her house she would treat it like one of her own children. She said the mother came and spent a few days at her house, and being satisfied that her boy would receive proper care, consented to leave him. The night before she was to leave him, the missionary said to the western lady: "I want to leave my boy tomorrow morning without a tear"; said she, "I may never see him again." But she didn't want him to think she was weeping for anything she was doing for the Master. The lady said to herself, "She won't leave that boy without a tear." But the next day, when the carriage drove up to the door, the lady went upstairs and said she heard the mother in prayer, crying, "O God, give me strength for this hour. Help me to go away from my boy without a tear." When she came down there was a smile upon her face. She hugged him and she kissed him, but she smiled as she did it. She gave up all her five or six children without shedding a tear, went back to India, and in about a year there came a voice, "Come up hither." Do you think she would be a stranger in the Lord's world? Don't you think she won't be known there, a mother that loved her God more than her children? When I think of that it seems as if I don't know much about making sacrifice for my Master. Oh, that we might know more about the love of Christ.

Sympathy

The next thing I want of speak of is sympathy. We have got to get into sympathy with people if we are going to do them good. This world wants sympathy about as much as anything. There are so many we could reach if we could sympathize with them. If we stand upon a higher plane, we won't succeed. The Son of God passed by the mansions and went down in a manger that he might sympathize with the lowly. If we want to reach people, we have got to put ourselves in the places of those people, if we are going to succeed.

People say, "How are the masses going to be reached?" Why, get into sympathy with them. If a man knows you are in sympathy with him, his heart, however hard it may be, will be broken. A gentleman one day came to my office for the purpose of getting me interested in a young man who had just got out of the penitentiary. Said the gentleman, "He says he doesn't want to go to the office, but I want your permission to bring him in and introduce him." I said, "Bring him in." The gentleman brought him in and introduced him. I took him by the hand, told him I was glad to see him, invited him up to my house, and when I took him into my family I introduced him as my friend. When my little daughter came into the room I said, "Emma, this is papa's friend." And she went up and kissed him, and the man sobbed aloud. After the child left the room I said, "What is the matter?" "O sir," he said, "I have not had a kiss for years. The last kiss I had was from my mother, and she was dying. I thought I would never love another one again." His heart was broken. Just that little kindness showed I was in sympathy with him.

Another young man, just out of the penitentiary, came to me and after I had talked with him for some time, he didn't seem to think I was in sympathy with him. I offered him a little money. "No," he said, "I don't want your money." "What do you want?" "I want someone to have confidence in me." I got down and prayed with him, and in my prayer I called him a brother and he shed tears the moment I called him brother. So if we are going to reach men we must make them believe we are their brothers.

We must put ourselves in their places. I tell you, if we only put ourselves in their places we can succeed in bringing souls to Christ. When we see a poor drunkard, let us bear in mind that we might have been in the same place under the same circumstances. O! may God give us love and sympathy so that we can reach the masses, and that many may be reached in this way, and we will see men coming to Christ by the thousands. I believe in my soul we are going to see the greatest work in New York we have ever seen in this world. Let every one of us that love the Lord Jesus Christ make up our minds that by the grace of God we will try to help some soul to Christ, and if that is our prayer, the Lord will make us wise in leading souls to him.

10

How to Study the Bible

JOHN 10:35-36

If he called them gods, unto whom the word of God came—and the scripture cannot be broken—what about the one whom the Father set apart as his very own and sent into the world?

One thing I have noticed in studying the word of God, and that is, when a man is filled with the Spirit, he deals largely with the word of God; whereas the man who is filled with his own ideas, refers rarely to the word of God. He gets along without it, and you seldom see it mentioned in his discourses.

A great many use the Bible only as a text-book. They get their text from the Bible, and go on without any further allusion to it; but when a man is filled with the word, as Stephen was, he cannot help speaking Scripture. Moses constantly repeated the commandments. Joshua, when he came across Jordan with his people, instructed that the law of the

Lord God be read. Christ constantly referred to the Bible, saying: "Thus saith the Scriptures."

Now, as old Dr. Bonner of Glasgow once said, "the Lord didn't tell Joshua how to use the sword, but he told him how he should meditate on the Lord day and night, and then he would have good success." When we find a man meditating on the words of God, my friends, that man is full of boldness and is successful. And the reason why we have so little success in our teaching is because we know so little of the word of God. You must know it and have it in your heart. A great many have it in their head and not in their heart. If we have the Spirit of God in our heart, then we have something to work upon. He does not use us because he is not in us. Mr. Sankey has been singing: "No word he hath spoken, Was ever yet broken."

As we find in our text, "the Scripture cannot be broken." There is a great deal of infidelity around, and it has crept into many of the churches, too. These doubters take up the Bible and wonder if they can believe it all—if it is true from back to back, and a good many things in it they believe are not true.

But do you think that if the Bible was a bad book it would make men good? Do you think if it was a false book it could make men good? We should be convinced that it is true. When we take it into our hands, let us know that it is the word of God and try to understand it. Many of the passages appear difficult to understand. But consider this: if we could understand it clearly from front to back immediately, it would be like any human book. The very fact that we cannot understand it all at once is the highest proof that it is the word of God.

Many people read the Bible as if it were simply another task. They say, "Well, I've read it through, I know all that's in it," and lay it aside. How many people prefer the morning paper? But the Bible is really the only newspaper. It tells us all that has taken place for the last six thousand years, and it tells us all the news of the future. Why, seventeen hundred years before Christ, it told the people of the coming of Christ. They knew he was coming. The daily papers could not tell them this. The articles may have been written by learned men—brilliant editorial-writers—but they couldn't tell us this. If you want news, study the Bible—the blessed old Bible—and you will find it has all the news of the world.

How to Study the Bible

Now we come to the question, "How should we study it?" A great many read it as I used to read it, just to ease my conscience. I had a rule before I was converted to read two chapters a day. If I failed to do so before I retired, I used to jump out of bed and read them. But if you asked me fifteen minutes later what I had read, I could not have told you. Now this is the trouble with many of us—we read with the head and not with the heart. A man may read his Bible, but when he has closed it you may ask him what chapter he read last, and he cannot tell you. He sometimes puts a mark in it to tell him; but without the mark he doesn't know where to start again—for his reading has been so careless. Just as I used to do when hoeing corn, I would put a stick in the furrow to mark the place where I had hoed last. A good many people are just like this. They pick up a chapter here, and there is no connection in their reading, and consequently they don't know anything about the word of God. If we want to understand the Bible we've got to study it—read it on our knees, asking the Holy Ghost to give us the understanding to see what the word of God is. If we go about it that way, and turn our face, as Joshua did, in prayer, and set ourselves to study these blessed and heavenly truths, the Lord will not disappoint us, and we will soon know our Bible, and when we know our Bible then it is that God can use us.

Three Essential Books

Let me say there are three books which every Christian ought to have. If you don't have them, go out and buy them before you get your tea. The first is a good Bible—a good large-print Bible. I don't like those little ones you can scarcely see. Get one in large print. A good many object to a large Bible because they can't carry it in their pocket. Well, if you can't carry it in your pocket, it is a good way to carry it under your arm. It is showing what you are—it is showing your flag. Now a great many of you are coming in from the country to these meetings, and when you get on the train you see people who are not ashamed to sit down and play cards. I don't see why the children of God should be ashamed of carrying their Bible under their arms in the cars.

"Ah!" some say, "That is the spirit of a Pharisee." It would be the pharisaical spirit if you hadn't dipped down into heavenly truths, if you haven't the Spirit of God with you. Suppose you read the daily papers a little less, and read the Bible a little oftener. Some say, "I haven't time." Take time. I don't believe there is a businessman in Chicago who couldn't find an hour a day to read his Bible if he wanted to.

The second book you need is a good concordance, and the third a scriptural textbook. Whenever you come to something in the word of God that you don't know, hunt for its meaning in those books. Suppose after the meeting I am looking all over the platform and Dr. Kittredge says: "What are you looking for?" and I answer, "Oh, nothing, nothing," and he would leave. If he thought I hadn't dropped anything he wouldn't stay. But suppose I had lost a very valuable ring which some esteemed friend had given me, and I told him this. He would stay with me, and we would move this organ, and those chairs, and look all over and by looking carefully, we would find it. If a man hunts for truths in the word of God, and reads it as if he was looking for nothing particular, he will get nothing.

Dig Deep

When the men went to California in the gold excitement, they went to dig for gold, and they worked day and night with a terrible energy just to get gold. Now, my friends, if they wanted to get the pure gold they had to dig for it, and when I was there I was told that the best gold was got by digging deep for it. So the best truths are got by digging deep for them.

When I was in Boston I went into Mr. Prang's chromo establishment. I wanted to know how the work was done. He took me to a stone several feet square, where he took the first impression, but when he took the paper off the stone I could see no sign of a man's face; the paper was just tinged. I said I couldn't see any sign of a man's face there. "Wait a little," he said. He took me to another stone, but when the paper was lifted I couldn't see any impression yet. He took me up, up to eight, nine, ten stones, and then I could see just the faintest outlines of a man's face. He went on till he got up to about the twentieth stone, and I could see the impression of a face, but he said it was not very correct yet. Well, he went on until he got up, I think, to the twenty-eighth stone, and a perfect face appeared, and it looked as if all it had to do was to speak and it would return my conversation. If you read a chapter of the Bible and don't see anything in it, read it a second time, and if you cannot see anything in it read it a third time. Dig deep. Read it again and again, and even if you have to read it twenty-eight times, do so, and you will see the man Christ Jesus, for he is in every page of the word, and if you take Christ out of the Old Testament you will take the key out of the word.

Study Both Old and New Testaments

Many in the churches nowadays are saying that they believe the teachings in the New Testament are to be believed, but those in the Old are not. Those who say this don't know anything about the New. There is nothing in the Old Testament that God has not already put his seal upon. "Why," some people say to me, "Moody, you don't believe in the flood. All the scientific men tell us it is absurd." Let them say what they will. Jesus tells us of it, and I would rather take the word of Jesus than that of any other one. I haven't got much respect for those who dig down for stones with shovels, in order to take away the word of God. Men don't believe in the story of Sodom and Gomorrah, but we have it sealed in the New Testament. "As it was in the days of Sodom and Gomorrah." They don't believe in Lot's wife, but he says, "Remember Lot's wife." So there is not a thing that men today cavil at but the Son of God endorses. They don't believe in the swallowing of Jonah. They say it is impossible that a whale could swallow Jonah—its throat is too small. They forgot that the whale was prepared for Jonah by God. We find that Christ endorses all the points in the Old Testament, from Genesis to Revelation. We have only one book—we haven't two. The moment a man begins to cut and slash away, it all goes. Some don't believe in the first five books. They would do well to look into the third chapter of John, where they will see the Samaritan woman at the well looking for the coming of Christ from the first five books of Moses.

I tell you, my friends, if you look for Christ, you will find him all through the Old Testament. You will find him in Genesis—in every book in the Bible. Just turn to Luke 24:27, you will find him, after he had risen again, speaking about the Old Testament prophets: "And beginning at Moses, and all the prophets, he expounded unto them in all the Scripture the things concerning himself." Concerning himself. Doesn't that settle the question? I tell you I am convinced in my mind that the Old Testament is as true as the New. "And he began at Moses and all the prophets." Mark that, "all the prophets." Then in the forty-fourth verse: "And he said unto them, these are the words which I spake unto you, while I was yet with you, that all things must be fulfilled which were written in the law of Moses and in the prophets and in the Psalms concerning me. Then opened he their understanding that they might understand the Scripture." If we take Christ out of the Old Testament what are you going to do with the Psalms and prophets? The book is a sealed book if we take away the New from it. Christ unlocks the Old and Jesus the New. Philip, in teaching the people, found Christ in the fifty-third chapter of Isaiah, "All we, like sheep, have gone astray; we have turned every one to his own way, and the Lord hath laid on him the iniquity of us all."

Why, the early Christians had nothing but the Old Testament to preach the gospel from—at Pentecost they had nothing else. So if there is any man or woman in this assembly who believes in the New Testament, and not in the Old, dear friends, you are deluded by Satan, because if you read the word of God you will find him spoken of throughout both books. If a man goes to cut up the Bible and comes to you with one truth and says, "I don't believe this and I don't believe that," it won't be long before he doubts it all.

Study One Book at a Time

Now the question is how to study the Bible. Of course, I cannot tell you how you are to study it; but I can tell you how I have studied it, and that may help you. I have found it a good plan to take up one book at a time. It is a good deal better to study one book at a time than to run through the Bible. If we study one book and get its key, it will, perhaps, open up others. Take up the book of Genesis, and you will find eight beginnings; or, in other words, you pick up the key of several books. The gospel was written that man might believe on Jesus Christ, and every chapter speaks of it. Now, take the book of Genesis; it says it is the book of beginnings. That is the key. Then the book of Exodus—it is the book of redemption; that is the key-word for the whole. Leviticus is the book of sacrifices. And so on through all the different books. Each one has its key.

We must also get rid of our biases. A great many people believe certain things. They believe in certain creeds and doctrines, and they run through the book to get Scripture in accordance with them. If a man is Calvinistic, for example, he wants to find something in the Bible in accordance with this doctrine. But if we go to seek truth the Spirit of God will come. Don't seek it in the light of Presbyterianism, or Methodism, or Episcopalianism, but study it in the light of Calvary.

Study One Word at a Time

Another way to study it is not only to take one book at a time; but I have been wonderfully blessed by taking up one word at a time. Take up the word and go to your concordance and find out all about it. I remember I took up the word "love," and turned to the Scriptures and studied it, and got so that I felt I loved everybody. I got full of it. When I went on the street I felt as if I loved everybody I saw. It ran out of my fingers. Suppose you take up the subject of love and study it. You will get so full of it that all you have got to do is to open your lips and a flood of the love of God will flow out.

If you go into a court you will find a lawyer pleading a case. He gets everything bearing upon one point, heaped up so as to carry his argument with all the force he can, in order to convince the jury. Now it seems to me a man should do the same in talking to an audience; just think that he has a jury before him, and he wants to convict a sinner.

Take the word "grace," for example. I didn't know what Calvary was until I studied grace. I got so full of God's wonderful grace that I had to speak. I had to run out and tell people about it. If you want to find out those heavenly truths take up the concordance and heap up the evidence, and you cannot help but preach. Take heaven; there are people all the time wondering what it is, and where it is. Take your concordance and see what the word of God says it is. Or do a study of the word "blood." Let those who are talking against blood look into the word of God, and they will find that if the Bible doesn't teach the blood it teaches nothing else. The word says, "The life of all flesh is in the blood, and without blood there is no remission." The moment a man talks against blood he throws out the Bible. Or take up Saul, and study him. You will find hundreds of men in Chicago just like him. Or study Lot.

Bible Study Is the Key to Revival

Let me say right here that if we are going to have, and I firmly believe in my soul that we are going to have, a revival in the Northwest—if we are going to have it, you must bring the people to the study of the word of God. I have been out here for a good number of years, and I am tired and sick of these spasmodic meetings; tired of the bonfires which, after a little, are reduced to a bundle of shavings. When I see men speaking to inquirers in the inquiry room without holding the word of God up to them, I think their work will not be lasting. What we want to do is to get people to study the word of God, in order that the work may be thorough and lasting. I notice when a man is brought coolly, and calmly, and intelligently, that man will have a reason for being a Christian. We must do that, we must bring people to the word of God if we don't want this western country filled with backsliders. Let us pray that we will have a scriptural revival, and if we preach only the word in our churches and in our Sunday schools, we will have a revival that will last to eternity.

Let us turn back to one of the Old Testament revivals, when the people had been brought up from Babylon. Look at the eighth chapter of Nehemiah: "And Ezra, the priest, brought the law before the congregation, both of men and women, and all that could hear with understanding, upon the first day of the seventh month, and he read therein, before the street that was before the water gate, from morning until midday, before the men and women and those that could understand, and the ears of the people were attentive unto the book of the law." There was no preaching. He merely read the word of God—that is, God's word—not man's. A great many of us prefer man's word to that of God.

We are running after eloquent preachers—after men who can get up eloquent moral essays. They leave out the word of God. We want to get back to the word of God.

They had an all-day meeting there, something like this, "and Ezra opened the book in the sight of all the people, for he was above all the people; and when he opened it all the people stood up." I can see the great crowd standing up to listen to the prophet, just like young robins taking in what the old robins bring them, "and Ezra blessed the Lord, the great God, and all the people answered, Amen, Amen. With lifting up their hands they bowed their heads and worshiped the Lord with their faces to the ground." "So they read the Law of God distinctly and gave the sense, and caused them to understand the reading."

The most important task of the preacher is to help people understand the word of God. It would be a great deal better if a preacher would sometimes stop and say, "Mr. Jones, do you understand that?" "No, I don't," and then the preacher might make it a little plainer, so that he could understand it. There would be a great difference in the preaching in some of the churches. He would talk a little less about metaphysics and science, and speak about something else. "Then he said unto them, go your way, eat the fat and drink the sweet, and send portions unto them for whom nothing is prepared, for this day is holy unto our Lord, neither be ye sorry, for the joy of the Lord is your strength."

If you will show me a Bible Christian living on the word of God, I will show you a joyful man.

He is mounting up all the time. He has got new truths that lift him up over every obstacle, and he mounts over difficulties higher and higher, like a man I once heard of who had a bag of gas fastened on either side, and if he just touched the ground with his foot over a wall or a hedge he would go; and so these truths make us so light that we bound over every obstacle.

Fill Yourselves with God's Word

Turn to that blessed old prophet Jeremiah. There was a time when he was not going to speak about the word of God any more. But when a man is filled with the word of God you cannot keep him still. If a man has got the word, he must speak or die. "Then I said, I will not make mention of him, nor speak any more in his name, but his word was in mine heart as a burning fire shut up in my bones, and I was weary with forbearing, and I could not stay." It set him on fire, and so a man filled with the word of God is filled as with a burning fire, and it is so easy for a man to work when he is filled with the word of God.

I heard of a man the other week who was going to preach about the blood of Christ. I was very anxious to see what he would say about it, and I got the paper next morning and I found there was nothing else there than scriptural quotations. I said that was the very best thing he could do. As we see in the twenty-third chapter of Jeremiah: "Is not my word like as a fire, saith the Lord, that breaketh the rock in pieces?" Those hard, flinty rocks will be broken if we give them the word of God. Those men in the Northwest that we cannot reach by our own words, give them this and see if they cannot be reached. Give people what God says and you will find it easy to preach. It seems to me if we had more of the word of God in our services and less of our own thoughts, there would be a hundred times more converted than there is. A preacher, if he wants to give his people the word, must have fed on the Word himself. A man must get water out of a well when there is water. He may dip his bucket in if it is empty, but he will get nothing.

I think the best thing I have heard in Chicago I heard the other day, and it has fastened itself upon my mind, and I must tell it to you ministers. We had for our subject in Farwell Hall the other day, the seventh chapter of John, when the Rev. Mr. Gibson said if a man was to come among a lot of thirsty men with an empty bucket they wouldn't come to him to drink. He said he believed that what was the trouble with most of the ministers was what had been the trouble with himself. He didn't have a bucket of living water, and the people wouldn't come to him to drink. Just look at an audience of thirsty men, and you bring in a bucket of clear sparkling water, and see how they will go for it. If you go into your Sunday schools and the children look into your buckets and see them empty, there is nothing for them there. So, my friends, if we attempt to feed others we must first be fed ourselves.

Mark Your Bibles

There is another thing which has wonderfully helped me. That is to mark my Bible whenever I hear anything that strikes me. If a minister has been preaching to me a good sermon, I put his name down next to the text, and then it recalls what has been said, and I can show it to others. You know we laymen have the right to take what we hear to one another. If ministers saw people doing this they would preach a good deal better sermons. Not only that, but if we understood our Bibles better, the ministers would preach better. I think if people knew more about the word than they do, so many of them would not be carried away with false doctrine.

There is no place I have ever been in where people so thoroughly understand their Bibles as in Scotland. Why, little boys could quote Scripture and take me up on a text. They have the whole nation educated, as it were, with the word of God. Infidelity cannot come there. A man got up in Glasgow at a corner, and began to preach universal salvation. "O sir," said an old woman, "that will never save the like of me." She had heard enough preaching to know that it would never save her. If a man comes among them with any false doctrine, these Scottish people instantly draw their Bibles on him. I had to keep my eyes open, and be careful what I said there. They knew their Bibles a good deal better than I did. And so if the preachers would get the people to read the word of God more carefully and note what they heard, there would not be so much infidelity among us.

Take your Bibles and mark them. Don't worry about wearing it out. It is a rare thing to find a man wearing his Bible out nowadays—and Bibles are cheap, too. You are living in a land where there are plenty. Study them and mark them, and don't be afraid of wearing them out. Now don't you see how much better it would be to study it? And if you are talking to a man—instead of talking about your neighbors—just talk about the Bible. When Christian men come together just compare notes, and ask one another: "What have you found new in the word of God since I saw you last?" Some men come to me and ask me if I have picked up anything new, and I give them what I have, and they give me what they have. An Englishman asked me some time ago, "Do you know much about Job?" "Well, I know a little," I replied. "If you've got the key of Job you've got the key to the whole Bible," he said. "What!" I replied; "I thought it was a poetical book." "Well," said he, "I will just divide Job into seven heads. The first is the perfect man—untried—and that is Adam and Eve before they fell. The second head is tried by adversity—Adam, after the fall. The third is the wisdom of the world—the three friends who came to try to help Job out of his difficulties. They had no power to help him at all. The fourth head takes the form of the Mediator, and in the fifth head God speaks at last. He heard him before by the ear, but he hears him now by the soul, and he fell down flat upon his face." A good many men in Chicago are like Job. They think they are mighty good men, but when they hear the voice of God they know they are sinners; they are in the dust. There isn't much talk about their goodness then. Here he was with his face down. Job learned his lesson. That was the sixth head, and in these heads were the burdens of Adam's sin. The seventh head was when God showed him his face. Well, I learned the key to the Bible. I cannot tell you how much this helped me. It could help you too.

Prayer-Meeting Talks 11

Evangelistic Services

A person said to me, "What do you mean by evangelistic services? Is not all service evangelistic? What do you mean by preaching the gospel? Are not all services in churches and all meetings preaching the gospel?" No. There is a good deal of difference.

There are three kinds of services—at least there ought to be—in every church, and everyone ought to keep them in their mind. There is worshiping God. That is not preaching the gospel at all. We come to the house of God to worship at times, when we meet around the Lord's table—that is worship, or ought to be. Then there is teaching—building up God's people. That is not preaching the gospel. Then there is proclaiming the good news of the gospel to the world, to the unsaved.

Now, the question we have before us is this, "How can these services be conducted to make them profitable?" Well, I should say you have to conduct them to interest the people. If they go to sleep, they certainly want to be roused up, and if one method doesn't wake them up, try another. But I think we ought to use our common sense, if you will allow me the word. We talk a good deal about common sense, but I think it is about the least sense we have, especially in the Lord's work. If one method doesn't succeed, let us try another. Preaching to empty seats just doesn't pay. If people won't come to hear us, let us go where they are. We want to preach. Go into some neighborhood and get some persons to invite you into their house, and get them into the kitchen, and preach there; but make it a point to interest the people, and as soon as they get interested they will follow you and fill the churches.

Now I have come to this conclusion, that if we are going to have successful gospel meetings, we have got to have a little more life in them. Life is found in singing new hymns, for instance. I know some churches that have been singing about a dozen hymns for the last twenty years, such hymns as "Rock of Ages" or "There Is a Fountain Filled with Blood." These hymns are good, but we need more variety. We want new hymns as well as old ones. I find it wakes up a congregation to bring in a new hymn now and then. And if you cannot wake them up with preaching, let us sing it into them. I believe the time is coming when we will make a good deal more of just singing the gospel. Then when a man is converted, have him give his testimony. Some people are afraid of that. I believe the secret of John Wesley's success was that he set every man to work as soon as he was converted. Of course you have to guard that point. Some say they become spiritually proud—no doubt of that; but if they don't go to work they become spiritually lazy.

Now, the first impulse of the young convert is to go and publish what Christ has done for him. Sometimes a young convert will wake up a whole community and a whole town, just merely by telling what the Lord has done for him; and it is good to bring in these witnesses and let them speak. Then another thing. In a good many towns where we have union meetings we change ministers every night, and a good many special religious meetings have been organized, and proved perfect failures. I am getting letters all the time telling about special meetings, how the people turned out well, but there were no results, and on inquiry I found they had a Methodist minister one night, a Baptist minister another, an Episcopalian minister another, a Congregational minister another, in order to keep all denominations in, and the result was they preached everybody out of doors. You could see right on the face of it that that would be the result. One man gets the people all interested, and just at the point where he needs to continue his own ministrations another steps in and he goes out. And so there is no getting hold of the people. Now I believe we have got to have one preacher.

I remember in Chicago, the last winter I was there, we had preaching every afternoon. We went out with invitations into saloons, billiard halls, etc., and we got a large audience there every afternoon, and we had a new minister every day. We wanted to bring in all denominations to keep harmony, and I believe there was one solitary conversion after preaching thirty days. If we had only stuck to one minister I believe we would have done a great work then and there. If we are going to have successful evangelistic services we cannot be changing speakers every night. And that is why it is best to get a man from out of town and all will unite around him. I wish we could get rid of this jealousy. If we could unite around one preacher and support him with our prayers and our money, if it need be, and just work with him, there would be results. I never knew it to fail yet. It is just this party feeling that comes in and prevents the good results we expect. We are afraid this denomination won't like it or that denomination won't be properly represented.

These meetings ought to be short. I find a great many are killed because they are too long. The minister speaks five minutes, and a minister's five minutes is always ten, and his ten minutes is always twenty, and the result is you preach everybody into the spirit and then out of the spirit before the meeting is over. When the people leave they are glad to go home, and ought to go home. When you send the people away hungry, they will come back again. There was a man in London who preached in the open air until everybody left him, and somebody said, "Why did you preach so long?" "Oh," said he, "I thought it would be a pity to stop while there was anybody listening." If we keep the meetings short, then people will come back again to hear.

Prayer Meetings

I have noticed, in traveling up and down the country and mingling with a great many ministers, that it is not the man that can preach the best that is the most successful, but the man who knows how to get his people together to pray. He has more freedom. It is so much easier to preach to an audience that is in full sympathy with you than to those who are criticizing all the time. It chills your heart through and through. Now, if we could only make our prayer meetings what they ought to be—so that people would attend, not out of any sense of duty, but because they delight to go—it would be a great help to a minister in his Sunday services. Now, I find it a great help in prayer-meetings to get the people right up close together, and then get myself right down among them. I believe many a meeting is lost by the people being scattered.

Another important thing is to see that the ventilation is good. Sometimes I have been in rooms where I think the air must have been in there five or six years. You cannot always trust the janitors to take care of it. The people get sleepy, and you think it is your fault. Very often such a thing is the fault of bad ventilation. See that you get fresh air—not too hot, and not too cold, but pure. Then it is a good thing to have a subject. Let all the people know a week beforehand what the subject is going to be. Take the subject of "faith," for example, and ask a brother or two privately to say a little on that subject. If they say, "I cannot get my thoughts together"; or, "I am so frightened when I get up that I tremble all over," then tell him just to get up and read a verse. It won't be long before they will add a few words to that verse, and after a while they will want to talk too much, and the meetings thus become very profitable to those men. What we want is variety. Instead of having Deacon Jones and Deacon Smith and Deacon Brown do all the praying and all the talking, have somebody else say something in this way, and thus create an interest.

I would not have the minister always take the lead, for I have noticed where the minister takes the lead, there is a collapse when he leaves. Now it seems to me a minister should get different ones into the chair, and when he leaves, the meetings won't miss him, and there will be no falling off. Not only that, but he is training his members to work. They will go out around the town and in schoolhouses, and preach the gospel, and we multiply preachers and workers in that way if they are only just taught to take part. Now I believe there are a great many in our church prayer meetings that could be brought out and made to be a great help if the ministers would only pay their attention to this. How many lawyers, physicians, public speakers do we have who do nothing to actively help along the work, and I believe that difficulty could be removed if the minister would make some effort to involve them. Let the father whose son has been converted get up and give thanks. Once in a while, have a thanksgiving meeting. It wakes up a church wonderfully, once in a while, to let the young converts relate their experiences. Then you say, what are you going to do with these men that talk so long? I would talk to them privately, and tell them they must try to be shorter. And it is a good thing sometimes for ministers themselves not to be too long. Sometimes they read a good deal of Scripture and talk until perhaps only fifteen minutes is left, and then they complain because Deacon Smith or Jones or someone else talks too long. Just let the minister strike the key note of the meeting, and if he can't do that in ten minutes he can't at all. Very often a minister takes up a chapter and exhausts it, and says everything he can think of in the chapter, and then wonders why a layman cannot add anything else to the study of the subject. Give out the subject a week ahead, let the minister take five or ten minutes in opening, and then let different ones take part. That would be greater variety. When a man takes part he gets greatly interested himself. It was pretty true what the old deacon said, that when he took part in the meetings they were very interesting, and when he didn't they seemed very dull.

Advice to Church Members

If ministers would encourage their members to be scattered among the audience, to never mind their pew but sit back by the door if need be, or in the gallery, where they can watch the faces of the audience, it would be a good thing. In Scotland I met a man who with his wife would go and sit among them, as they said, to watch for souls. When they saw anyone who seemed impressed they would go to him after the meeting and talk with him. Nearly all the conversions in that church during the last fifteen months had been made through that influence. Now, if we could only have from thirty to fifty laymen and laywomen, members of the church, whose business it is just to watch and afterwards to clinch them in. The best way in our regular churches is to let the workers all help pull the net in. You will get a good many more fishes—not one now and then but scores and scores. A stranger coming into a church likes to have someone speak to him. He does not feel insulted at all. A young man coming to New York a stranger and going to church, if someone asks him to go into the inquiry room, it makes him happy and cheers him. Two young men came into our inquiry room here the other night, and after a convert had talked with them, and showed them the way, the light broke in upon them. They were asked, "Where do you go to church?" They gave the name of the church where they had been going. Said one, "I advise you to go and see the minister of that church." They said, "We don't want to go there any more; we have gone there for six years and no one has spoken to us."

A man was preaching about Christians recognizing each other in heaven, and someone said, "I wish he would preach about recognizing each other on earth." In one place where I preached there was no special interest. I looked over the great hall of the old circus building where the meetings were being held, and saw men talking to other men here and there. I said to the secretary of the Young Men's Christian Association who had sponsored the meeting, "Who are these men?" He said, "They are a band of workers." They were all scattered through the hall, preaching and watching for souls. Out of the fifty of them, forty-one of their number had got a soul each and were talking and preaching with them. We have been asleep long enough. When the laity wake up and try and help the minister the minister will preach better. If the minister finds he has not been drawing the net right, if a good many in his church go to work and help him he will do better; he will prepare the sermons with that one thing in view: will this draw men to Christ?

I do not see how men can preach without inquiry meetings. I like to see the converts. One minister in Scotland said he did not believe in disturbing the impression. If he had made an impression he did not want anyone to say anything. He said, "After you sow the seed you don't want to go and dig it up to see whether it has sprouted." But I told him, "The farmers all harrow it in after it is sowed."

Advice to Christians

One thing has been laid upon my mind in the last hour, and that is, that we should pray to God to fill us with the Spirit. We have had a good many questions asked us by the young converts about how they should go to work. There is a great deal of work done by people who do not have the power of the Spirit; and to work without the power is like beating against the air.

I would call your attention to one thought: the gift of the Spirit is for service. We may be sons and daughters without power. God has a great many children that have not got any power. Their words are idle words; they might just as well speak in an unknown tongue; their speech is "as sounding brass and a tinkling cymbal." I suppose many of us have felt what it is to be preaching as though we were preaching to the air, our own hearts not moved, nor anyone else's either. When you go home, take your Bible for an hour or two, and study this one subject: the gift of the Holy Ghost for service. In the fourth chapter of Luke, verse eighteen, we read: "The Spirit of the Lord is upon me, because he hath anointed me to preach the gospel." It was after the Spirit came upon him that he commenced his ministry. Then he went back to Nazareth, and his work was blessed.

In the twentieth chapter of John, we find these words: "And when he had said this he breathed on them and said unto them, Receive ye the Holy Ghost." Of course his disciples had been converted before this. Back in the seventh chapter of John we find him saying on that great day of the feast, "If any man thirst let him come unto me and drink. He that believeth on me, out of his belly shall flow rivers of living water. Greater works than I have done you shall do, because I come of the Father, and the Holy Ghost shall be upon you which also comes of him."

If we are imbued with power from on high, it will then be ours to work for God. You cannot get water out of a dry well. You may pump and pump and pump, and the old machine will squeak, but there no water will come. Sometimes pumps are dry and you can't make any water come until you pour in a little at the top. So we have got to have water poured on us, or we cannot get any more power than a dry pump. What we want is this water of the Spirit poured upon ourselves. Oh, may he pour it upon us this afternoon.

Some people think because they have had the Holy Ghost resting upon them at one time in power, that Spirit is going to remain. But, I tell you, many a man that got converted and received the Holy Ghost, and was used ten years ago for the service of the Lord, has not got the power that he once had. He may be a good Christian, but he has lost the power. The people in his church know it. They say to each other, "What has come over our pastor?" He has not got the unction, he has not got the Holy Ghost. Oh, shall we not seek and pray for it here today? May the God of heaven breathe upon us one breath from the upper world before we go hence! In the second chapter of Acts, we read that Christ told his disciples to go back to Jerusalem and tarry there until they were imbued with power from on high. Those men had already been converted.

My friends, I think all too often we do not tarry at Jerusalem until we get the power. We forget about the Holy Ghost, and about the necessity of our being anointed for service. These very men that he breathed upon then were afterwards filled with the Holy Ghost, as we read in the fourth chapter of Acts. Peter and James and John had not remained full. We are greatly mistaken in thinking that we may remain satisfied with past mercies of grace that God gave us away back some ten years ago. We do not love the fresh manna.

While I was in England I met a minister whose health had become so poor that he had to get an assistant to help him preach. He could only preach once a week, and not always that. One day, in meeting, the Spirit of God came upon him anew, and he got freshly anointed. He came down to London a year afterwards and told me that during the past year he had preached eight sermons a week. He said he had never been so well in all his life. I believe it is not work that breaks down our health; it is pumping without the water! What we want to do is just to wait on God until he gives it to us. I know a minister who told me he felt that he was preaching without this anointing, and he felt that his sermons had not been blessed for a long long time. I know it was my own experience. I never like to talk about myself—it always makes me feel like a fool, but this may do some of you some good.

About four years ago I got into a cold state. It did not seem as if there was any unction resting upon my ministry. For four long months God seemed to be showing me myself. I found I was ambitious; I was not preaching for Christ; I was preaching for ambition. I found everything in my heart that ought not to be there. For four months, a wrestling went on within me, and I was a miserable man. But after four months the anointing came. It came upon me as I was walking in the streets of New York. Many a time I have thought of it since I have been here. At last I had returned to God again, and I was wretched no longer. I almost prayed, in my joy, "Oh, stay thy hand!" I thought this earthen vessel would break. He filled me so full of the Spirit.

If I have not been a different man since, I do not know myself. I think I have accomplished more in the last four years than in all the rest of my life. But it was preceded by a wrestling and a hard struggle. I thought I would never escape my miserable selfishness. There was a time when I wanted to see my little vineyard blessed but I could not get out of it. Now, I could work for the whole world. I would like to go around the world and tell the perishing millions of a Savior's love.

If in these closing meetings here we could get baptized by the Holy Ghost, would it not be blessed? Is there not a hungering and a thirsting to be filled today? "Blessed are they that hunger and thirst after righteousness, for they shall be filled." There is the word of the Lord Jesus. Is he not here today? Is not he able to fill us? If he would imbue us all, and expel all jealousy and sectarianism, would it not be blessed? He can conquer this earthly will and fill us with the Holy Ghost as were the early Christians. Your congregations will find your new anointing out, if you take the grace and the anointing away with you. They will say to each other directly, "What does it mean? What has come over our minister?" Oh, God grant that self may lose its interest for us today, and that Jesus may burst upon us with a new view; that we may behold him today as we never yet beheld him; and may he give us fresh anointing!

Christ the Good Samaritan

Luke 10:25

In this picture we get the whole gospel. Jerusalem was the city of peace. Jericho was a city condemned. From one to the other was down a long hill—an easy road to go, as the unfortunate man thought when he started on his journey. But he fell among thieves, who stripped him and left him half dead, and the priest and the Levite passed him by. These two men represent a large class of people. We can imagine the priest asking himself, "Am I my brother's keeper?" and complaining, "What did he want to go down there for any way? Why didn't he stay at home? He was a great deal better off in Jerusalem—he might have known something would happen to him." Some people think they have done their duty when they blame the poor for their poverty, and the unfortunate for the accidents which happen to them.

There is another class who always want to philosophize the minute they see any suffering. "Why does God allow these things? Why does he have sin and poverty in the world, I would like to know? He needn't have it; he could just as well made a world without it."

But here comes the Good Samaritan; he does more than pity and philosophize: he helps—gives oil and lifts the poor fellow on his beast. He is not afraid to touch him. He doesn't stop to ask whether he is a Jew or Gentile, or just what he is going to do with the man if he takes him away from there. Now a great many people ask us, "What are you going to do with these young converts when you get them? Where will you put them—into what church—Methodist, Baptist, Episcopal?" "Well, we don't know; we have not thought of that; we are trying to get them out of the ditch first." "Oh, well then, we don't want to have anything to do with it; we want it to be done decently and in order if we are going to have a hand in it."

These people are no Samaritans. They won't have anything to do with the poor fellows by the wayside if they cannot dispose of them ever afterwards to suit themselves. Let us not condemn those who have fallen into the ditch. Christ is our Good Samaritan; he has done everything for us and he tells us to do the same for others.

Create a Clean Heart in Me

Psalm 51:10

It seems as if here is where we might well stop and ask: Is our heart clean in the sight of God? Has he renewed a right spirit within us? Do we show that in our home, in our daily life, in our business, and in our contact with others? If we do not, it seems to me it is better to be praying for ourselves than for others, that the world may see that we have been with God's Spirit. If we are a great way from Christ in all our ways, our words will be cold and empty, and we cannot reach the world. There is power enough in this room to move all New York if we had the right spirit and clean hearts.

A friend of mine told me he had been preaching some time without seeing any results in his church, and he began to cry to God that he might have a blessing in his church. He said weeks went on and the answer didn't come, and he felt as if he must either have a blessing or give up the ministry. He must have souls or die. On one Sunday he threw himself on his knees in his study and cried to God: "O God, break this heart of mine and give me a contrite spirit." Just at this moment he heard a faint rap at the door, and opening it, his little child, four years old, entered. She had heard her father's prayer, and she said, "Father, I wish you would pray for me, I want a clean heart." "And," said he, "God broke my heart, and at the next meeting there were forty inquirers, after that one sermon." Oh, that our hearts may be tender, and may we know what it is to have broken hearts and contrite spirits.

How to Pray

2 Chronicles 4

The reason why so many prayers go unanswered is that they are either not in accordance with the will of God or because we have not been sufficiently cleansed from our sins. Some secret sin may be clustering around our hearts which he wants removed first. John in his Gospel tells us that it is a comfort that if we ask anything according to his will it will be received. But some will say, "Well, how am I to know what is the will of God?" In Romans 8:6 we read: "Likewise the Spirit also helpeth our infirmities: for we know not what we should pray for as we ought; but the Spirit itself maketh intercession for us with groanings which cannot be uttered." In Luke 11:1 we read: "And it came to pass that one of his disciples said unto him, Lord, teach us how to pray as John also taught his disciples." I have no doubt many persons here have said, "Lord, teach me how to pray." I'd rather be able to pray like Daniel than to preach like David. The world knows little of the works wrought by prayer. But our words at the best seem empty and cold. Christ replied to the disciple, "When ye pray, say, Our Father which art in heaven, hallowed be thy name." Later he says, "Ask and it shall be given to you."

The Three Classes of Christians

There are three classes of Christians: the asking, the seeking, and the knocking Christians. There are a good many in the first class. They are continually asking but do not seek. If you will allow me the expression, they run away from the mercy seat before God has had time to answer them. Then there are the seeking Christians, who are a step. They always try to find out what God wants them to do, and where the trouble lies within themselves. There is not a Christian on the face of the earth who, if he enters upon this self-examination, will fail to find that when his prayers are not answered there is something in his own heart which he cherishes but should give up. Lastly we have the knocking Christians. This is the class we want here. If you knock "it shall be opened," and we should keep knocking until it is. When the Holy Ghost is upon us, how everyone longs to speak and to work for God! Let us ask for great things—that God may fill us with the Holy Spirit, and we may learn to do his will.

We don't know how to pray. Unless the Spirit of God be with us, we cannot expect that our prayers will be answered. Many are asking for what would be an injury to them should God grant it. God knows what we want better than we. He knows when anything would injure us, should we have it, and it is because he loves us that many prayers are unanswered. We sometimes fail to see why God withholds certain gifts, but later in life we will understand it. I well remember how I wanted many things some years ago, and can plainly see that they might have been a positive injury to me. Children ask many things of their parents, but the parent does not always grant their requests. We love them too well to give what would harm them. So it is with God and our prayers.

I want to call your attention to the third chapter of Deuteronomy, where prayers were uttered which were not answered. Moses wanted to cross the Jordan. He was praying for himself. It was no sign God did not love him because he did not answer that prayer. He loved Moses as he did no other man of that time. He took him up to a mountain, let him die as it were on his breast and then buried him. After fifteen hundred years that prayer was answered. He was over Jordan on the mountain with Elias. And there was Elijah, who prayed that he might die. But wasn't it better for Elijah to go to heaven in that chariot of fire? Yes. God loved him too much to let him die. It is a good deal better to let God choose than to choose ourselves.

Confessing Our Sins

Daniel 9

It is when we confess our sins that we have power within. It was when Abraham was down in the dust that God talked with him. If we have not confessed our own sins, it is no time to urge others to come to Christ. Should we attempt it, they might say to us, "Physician, heal thyself. Get the beam out of thine own eye." If a man is irritable in his own house, and fails to manifest the doctrine of Christ in his own life, it is useless for him to talk with others. It will help us, as workers in God's vineyard, if we drop the "you" in our conversation, and say "we." There is power enough in this hall to move all of

New York, if only we were aroused to the work, and were all right in our own hearts. There may be some secret sin lurking around our hearts which we need to get rid of. There is no room for pride, self, and worldliness in the hearts of those filled with the Spirit. It isn't preaching that we want. You've had preaching enough to convert all New York, and it's good preaching. You have intellectual power in your pulpits—perhaps you never had more. But what you all need is the power of prayer.

We must confess to God, for we are sinners against him. It's not to man that we must confess. We haven't sinned against him. I know of only one instance mentioned in the Bible where a man confessed his sins to men, and that was Judas, and he went out and hanged himself. Oh, let us have more of the spirit of confession in our prayers. A man often wonders why his prayer isn't answered, and asks, "Hasn't God said that whatever we ask for we shall receive?" Yes, God has said this, but there are conditions under which he will grant our requests. One is that we should forgive others, as we would have God forgive us. If there is a soul on the face of the earth that you can't forgive, there is no use of praying. Your prayers will be mere mummeries. We must follow the words of Christ: "If ye abide in me." And we must have faith. Christ tells us how we can move mountains, if we have faith. And the last condition I would mention is that we ought always to pray, and never to faint. Earnest and continued supplications bring the blessings.

Disobedience

All the trouble in the world originates in this one little word. It is the cause of all misery, and is the open door through which it comes. It was there that Adam fell; God told him that he shouldn't do a certain thing, and he did it. In the fifteenth chapter of 1 Samuel we read of sacrifices and obedience, and that God prefers being obeyed to having any sacrifice offered that men may choose. The first thing that God wants is obedience. That's what we want in our families. If our children disobey us there comes an alternative. They must learn to obey, or one of them must leave the house. It is the same with the kingdom of God. If we enter it we must obey. To obey is better than making sacrifice.

Saul lost his crown, his throne, his son, and his friend Samuel, and the friendship of his son-in-law David; he turned his back on them all because of his disobedience, and he finally lost his life. But that other Saul, over in the New Testament, was obedient unto death. He had no Jonathan, save at the right hand of God. He had no crown, no throne, but he won them both. A blessing is promised to all who will obey. God deals with individuals as with nations. The punishment is the same.

A crisis may come when we do not know whether to obey God or our employers or possibly our parents. The word of God makes the way clear. When we come into God's kingdom, "whatsoever he saith to thee, do it." If the laws of the nation are in conflict with God's law, they must be broken.

When those in the army disobey orders, they are court-martialed and shot. No one complains. Now, my friends, is there not as much reason why we should obey the orders of heaven, and, when we do not, should we not be punished? Sinners are willing to do anything but obey God. Coming to him as a poor beggar is what they don't like. If they could buy salvation they would gladly do it. Some men down on Wall Street, I fancy, would pay great prices. Many people come to me and say, "Mr. Moody, is it right for me to go to the theater? Can I dance?" The real question, however, is this: Can we glorify God by doing such thing? It's a good deal better to be right with God. Then he will look down with pleasure and bless us.

Hope

If I should question everyone here today I have no doubt each would be found with a hope. But is it a true or a false hope? If it is false it is worse than none. Job spoke about the hypocrite, and said: "Will God hear his cry when trouble cometh upon him?" Solomon wrote in Proverbs that "the hope of the unjust man shall perish." If you have false hopes of heaven, the best thing you can do is to give them up. For what are they good for? Will they bear you over Jordan? Will they sustain you beyond the grave? But true hope is not in regard to eternal life. That is secured to us if we are born of God.

Our hopes are of the resurrection of Christ, his second coming and our own resurrection. It is written, "He that believeth hath eternal life." The Lord himself shall descend from heaven, the dead shall be raised, and we shall meet him in the air. It is a glorious hope. All that believe shall rise. That is a hope sure and steadfast. Someone says that joy is like a lark that sings in the morning, but hope is like a nightingale that sings in the night. We won't need hope after we get to heaven. But hope takes us there. You can have Christ and this hope today if you will. "He came to his own and his own received him not, but as many as received him to them gave he power."

Joy
Galatians 5:22

Love is the first fruit. If we don't love our enemies we're not converted. We must be able to forgive others before God will forgive us. There is no grace in loving our friends and those who love us. The greatest heathen would do that.

But joy is what we want to talk about today. No man is converted who does not have joy. The angels said, "I bring you good tidings of great joy." The world may give happiness, but it is fleeting. It may vanish in a day. But joy comes from heaven; it is a river, and flows on forever from the throne.

Some people say they once had this joy, but do not have it now. Let them turn over to the words, "Restore to me the joy of thy salvation." He will do it. But remember the words, "Study the word and work." A man may work and still not have joy, and he may study the Bible and not have it. He must work and study both. Then it will come, "The joy of the Lord is your strength." If you have joy in your heart you can't help but work. Your strength will not fail you.

There are three kinds of joy. First is the joy of our salvation. How well we remember the day when we found the Lord! "Happy day"—how we like to sing that hymn! Then there is the joy of seeing others converted. I pity those who keep out of the inquiry room. We who are in there get the cream of this work; while you, if I may be allowed the expression, only get the skimmed milk. And a third kind of joy is that which comes from seeing others walk in God's ways. In John 15:11 Christ says, "These things have I spoken unto you, that my joy might remain with you and your joy might be full." That was better than if he had left us silver and gold. That's his legacy, his will. Yes, "My joy I leave with you" and thank God the devil can't get hold of it; the world can't take it away. How easy it is to save souls when you have joy in your heart. The world sees it in our faces. Last night we had the most extraordinary meeting that has been held. It was the grandest impression I have had in New York, to see those young men standing up. Ah, the joy of Christ was on their faces.

Christ

John 4:11–12

If Christ was not divine, he was not a Savior, and we are man-worshipers; all our hopes are gone, and our faith is vain. Matthew wrote to prove that Christ is the true Messiah, the Son of David. Mark begins with Malachi, where the Old Testament leaves off. Luke begins with Zechariah. But John sweeps over them all, and goes back to the bosom of God, and brings Christ from the throne.

The eleventh and twelfth verses of the fourth chapter of John are to me two of the most precious in the Bible. They are about worn out in my Bible with use: "*And he came unto his own, and his own received him not; but unto such as believed on him, to them gave he power.*" Mark the "him." There is no creed, no denomination, no system required. There is not a soul here but can take him today if they will. "Whomsoever" has been said, and it means all mankind. We have the best reasons to believe that this religion is true. How could hundreds of thousands of Christians have found so much comfort in Christ if it were all a myth? See how men have been elevated and lifted up. Let us only take God at his word and we will be saved.

Last night in the young men's meeting, a young man stood up and told how he had been saved three years ago; how his mother and sisters had all given him up, and the Lord reached down and lifted him into life. Isn't this proof of the Lord's power? All who find Christ tell the same story, be they American, English, German, Chinese, or of other nationality. What more proof do you want than this? There is much discussion today about miracles. But isn't a conversion a miracle? John's Gospel reminds us to "believe, believe, believe." That idea is ever before John. Every chapter but two in his writings mentions it. God doesn't tell you to feel; many say they don't feel right to come to Christ. God tells you to believe. You must trust him first. You must have faith in him before you can have Christian experience. "Though he slay me, yet will I trust him"; that's it. If he doesn't save us, who can? All the churches and priests in the world can't do it. Now let us pray that all the unbelief in this building may be swept away.

Praise

I think this is the first praise meeting we have had. We have been praying a great deal, and now let us praise God. There is much more said in the Bible about praise than about prayer. The Psalms are nothing but praise, and as David got nearer the end of his journey he seems to have thought of little else. So it is with Christians—the nearer they get to heaven the more they praise God. The saints praise him in heaven, and men should learn how to praise him here below. Everything that God has created except the heart of man, praise him. The sun, moon, and stars, praise him, and Oh, let us praise him. "Praise the Lord, O my soul," says the Psalmist.

I knew a man who always used to praise God under any circumstances. One day he came in with a severe cut on his finger, and said, "I have cut my finger. Praise God! I didn't cut it off." Under all circumstances let us praise God that our misfortunes are no worse. Let us ask him to help us to praise him. If we only had more of these praise-meetings, I think it wouldn't be long before a glorious revival would sweep through all the churches. Forget your troubles, and begin to praise God today.

Christ Mighty to Save

The key note of this meeting is the sentiment of that hymn: "Christ Mighty to Save." I have had considerable experience with men enslaved by strong drink. They try often to reform, but seldom succeed alone. The reason is that they have too much confidence in their own strength. When they give that up, and learn to trust alone in Christ, they are saved. When they call on God for help, they always get it. If we could only save ourselves by our own strength there would be no need of a Savior. The worst enemy man has is himself. His pride and self-confidence often ruin him. They keep him from trusting to the arms of a loving Savior. We are wicked by our nature; there is nothing good in us; the Bible teaches us that all the way through. David in the Psalms said: "There is none that doeth good; no, not one."

He was right. We are all evil in our nature. It is the old Adam. I tell you man without God is a failure, and a tremendous failure. There's nothing good in him. It is a great deal better to believe God than to hope for salvation through your own poor exertions. How many times have you resolved to break off from some habit and failed! The heart is deceitful and desperately wicked. What we need is a new creation. Don't try to patch up your old natures. We need to be regenerated.

Promises of the Bible

There was a man in London who had all the promises of God printed together in a little book, and some time after someone in the country sent up for a copy. He received the answer that all the promises of God were out of print. Perhaps that man had never heard of the Bible.

At one time in Chicago, when the meetings grew a little dull, I told them we would go through the Bible and look for all the promises God had given us. From that time there were no more dull meetings. We had never realized before what promises God has made to those who believe in Jesus Christ. When I was traveling in the West, I met a man on the train who was marking a lot of notes he had in his hand with the letters B, G, P, and so on, and I asked him what it was for. He said some of them were bad, the parties were bankrupt, and he never expected to collect them. Some were good, though the men were slow to pay, and some were only possibly good, and he marked them to calculate his chances. Now some people are just like this with God's promises; some they expect will be kept, and some they do not; some are barely possible. I advise you to mark all of God's promises as good. God always keeps every promise he makes. I defy any infidel to show any promise he has not kept.

Peace
Numbers 6:26

The gospel is a gospel of peace, and our God is a God of peace, not of contention. The wicked know nothing of peace. There is no peace saith the Lord, for the wicked; they are like the troubled sea—but you don't need to go to the Bible to find that out. If you will look around you, you will see it. If you have not got peace, it is a sure sign that you have not found the true God, for the peace of God will keep your hearts and minds if you have found him. Look in Numbers 6:26: "The Lord lift up his countenance upon thee, and give thee peace." The Lord will keep thee; the Lord will give thee peace; the Lord will bless thee—blessing at the foundation, blessing on the top, peace in the middle, solid, real peace such as the world cannot give or take away. When a man has left a will, how eagerly we read it! We don't care much for a dry law paper, but if it has got our name in it with a legacy we never find it dry. Now God says, "My peace I leave with you." O child of God have you got it? None of us have enough of it. I get angry and disturbed and make a fool of myself very often; I wish I had peace enough to keep me from it, but God gives good measure, shaken up, pressed down, full measure. Let our hearts be open to receive the peace of God.

Affliction

Psalm 119:67, 71

"Before I was afflicted I went astray; but now have I kept thy word"; and again, "It is good for me that I have been afflicted, that I might learn thy statutes." We can stand affliction better than we can prosperity, for in prosperity we forget God. When our work is light, our prospects good, and everything looks smooth and easy, we are more apt to give ourselves over to pleasure. Somebody said: "It is the dead level of affairs that makes us go to ruin." A great many have a wrong idea of God, and think he sends afflictions because he doesn't love them; they think that because they don't know him. He sends afflictions to humble our hearts and make us look to him, and because he loves us, so he cannot let us leave him and forget him.

Belief in God

2 Kings 7

I have believed in God now for thirty years. When first converted I did not believe in him very much, but ever since then I have believed in him, more and more every year. When people come to me, tell me they can't believe, and ask what they shall do, I tell them to do as I once knew a man to do. He went and knelt down and told God honestly he could not believe in him. So I advise them to go off alone and tell it right out to the Lord. But if you stop to ask yourself *why* you don't believe in him, is there really any reason? People read infidel books and wonder why they are unbelievers. I ask why they read such books. They think they must read both sides. I say that book is a lie, how can it be one side when it is a lie? It is not one side at all.

Suppose a man tells lies about my family, and I read them so as to hear both sides; it would not be long before some suspicion would creep into my mind. I said to a man once, "Have you got a wife?" "Yes, and a good one." I asked, "Now what if I should come to you and cast out insinuations against her?" And he said, "Well, your life would not be safe long if you did." I told him to treat the devil as he would treat a man who went round with such stories. We are not to blame for having doubts flitting through our minds, but for harboring them. Let us go out trusting the Lord with heart and soul today.

Christ Came to Save Sinners

"They that are whole need not a physician, but they that are sick. I come not to call the righteous but sinners to repentance."

Matthew, Mark, and Luke all give an account of this saying of Christ's—that he came to save sinners. Sin may keep us out of heaven, but cannot keep us from coming to Christ. Christ was a physician; he came to save sinners, and he never lost a case that was brought to him. If you should call a physician to see a friend and he should go and find that man was perfectly well, he would be indignant, wouldn't he?

I remember when I was in Chicago, seeing the advertisement of a patent medicine stuck all round on houses and rocks and fences. "Pain Killer! Pain Killer! Pain Killer!" and I thought, "There is a man who is bound to make some money." I hadn't any pain I wanted cured, so I did not pay much attention to it. But one morning when spring came I had a headache, and when I saw that this Pain Killer would cure headache I bought a bottle. Men don't want a doctor until they are sick, and don't go to Christ until they feel their need of him. It is no use to offer bread to a man who is not hungry, or water to a man who is not thirsty. "They that are whole need not a physician, but they that are sick." Paul said he was the chief of sinners, and if the chief is saved, there is hope for every sinner.

Joseph of Arimathea

What I want to call attention to this morning is how one act done for Christ, with a pure motive, will live forever. All four of the disciples give an account of this deed. Joseph of Arimathea was a rich man and a counselor, a good and just man, and

John tells us he had long been a secret disciple of Christ. He had never come out boldly for fear of the Jews, but in that hour, when all had deserted him and one had betrayed him, the death of Christ brought Joseph out, and he alone came forward to care for the crucified body.

It is the death of Christ which should enlist us all. The fact that he died for us should make us all come forward to advance his kingdom. Joseph had been opposed to the death of Jesus, but he had taken no part in his trial and crucifixion. Dr. Bonner says, when you have a trial before a committee and one of its members will oppose the measure you want to carry you don't send for him—you have the meeting without him if you can. So when this matter came up before the Sanhedrin, Joseph was not there and was not sent for. It is only when Christ was dead upon the cross that Joseph came forward as a disciple and begged the body from Pilate—an act which has lived nearly one thousand nine hundred years, and which will continue to live throughout all time.

Matthew, Mark, and Luke do not tell us where Joseph got the myrrh and aloes, but John tells us that Nicodemus brought a hundred pounds weight, and that they put linen clothes upon the body of Jesus with the spices, and laid it in a new sepulchre wherein was never a man yet laid. It was a tomb Joseph had built for himself, expecting to lie there some day, but he probably thought the sepulchre would be all the sweeter if Christ had lain there.

Losing Sight of Self
Mark 9

There is no doubt but hundreds of Christians who have attended these meetings wonder how they can now go out and work for the Lord. There is one thing necessary first, and that is we must lose ourselves and think only of duty. In this chapter which I have just read, we learn how the disciples had disputed among themselves who should be the greatest; but Christ said to them, "If any man desire to be first, the same shall be last of all and servant of all." If a man wants to become wise before God, he must be willing to appear a fool before the world. God doesn't want our wisdom, he wants our ignorance. We read in the tenth chapter of Mark, thirty-first verse, "But many that are first shall be last, and the last first." Then Jesus tells of seven things that are going to happen in reference to his death. "The Son of Man shall be delivered unto the chief priests, and they shall condemn him to death, and shall deliver him to the Gentiles; and they shall mock him, and shall scourge him and shall spit upon him, and shall kill him, and the third day he shall rise again."

This was a prophecy, and I have an idea that many things which we still think are visionary will literally take place at some remote time. Yet right after this prophecy the disciples said to him, "Master, we would that thou shouldst do for us whatsoever we shall desire." Here is self emerging again. It was the dying request of Christ that we should eat of the bread and drink of the wine in remembrance of him; yet many young converts say to me, "I need not go to the Communion table, need I?" I tell them they need not go unless they want to, but if that was the dying request of any friend they had they would be willing to do it all their lives; why, then, should they not desire to do it in remembrance of their Savior? They never thought of it in that way, they say. We want to be remembered in heaven, and Christ wants to be remembered here. We must pray to God to fill us with this spirit, and help us get rid of self; and never let us stop and try to think who shall be greatest.

True Friendship

2 Samuel 15

David was fleeing in exile from Jerusalem. Absalom had already undermined his power and superseded him on the throne. But as David went through the gate six hundred men passed on before him, and the king said to Ittai, the leader: "Wherefore goest thou also with us; return to thy place and abide with the king, for thou art a stranger and also an exile." And Ittai answered the king and said, "As the Lord liveth, and as my lord the king liveth, surely in what place my lord the king shall be, whether in death or life, even there also will thy servant be." There was another man, too, called Hushai, who went out to meet the king, but he returned again to the city. How it must have pleased

David to have found Ittai outside the gate. Ittai is worth thousands of Hushais. David did not know who his friends were until trouble came. There was true fellowship, true love in that act. In time of distress Ittai would not desert his king, but followed him into exile. So it should be in the church. That is just what Christ looks for; the only thing which can please him is the true love that will leave all to follow him. Some people do not know the meaning of the word "fellowship"—it means partnership. Our partnership is with Christ the Son, and when we come into it everything we have belongs to the firm; we can do nothing by ourselves without consulting Christ. We must be like Ittai, willing to leave the city and all we possess, if necessary, to follow him.

Our Refuge

I want to call your attention to the six cities of refuge appointed by Joshua for the children of Israel. These cities were set apart that all men who killed any person unawares or unwittingly, and without hatred, might flee to them and be safe within their gates. The magistrates had to see to it that guide-boards were put up, stones cleared away, and the roads kept clear for those who fled for their lives from the avengers of blood. These ancient cities of refuge are in our day represented by Christ. He is our refuge in all times of trouble.

The names of the cities are Hebrew, and all have a meaning. *Kadesh* means holiness. If we flee to this city of refuge we will be made holy. Had Christ committed sin we could have no hope, but since he is without sin, if we are in Christ we are made perfect. *Shechem* meant shoulder, which means strength and power. If a man needs strength he must flee there. Sins are in one of two places, on us or on Christ. If we are weak we must find strength in Shechem. *Hebron* means joined. If we can get there we are joint heirs with Jesus Christ. *Beser* means fortified; you are secured there if you want to get away from the world. *Ramoth* means heights and *Golan* means exile—exile in this world and citizenship in heaven. These six cities ought to be a help to you. Have we Christ for our refuge? If a man is away from God what hope has he? It is folly for a man who has an appetite for drink to try and overcome it by himself; he can't overcome both his appetite and the devil alone. It is only through Christ that we can be secure.

The Holy Spirit

If we have the Spirit, we have the fruit of the Spirit. If the Spirit of God is in us, we will have these qualities of his Spirit. "He that loveth not, knoweth not God; for God is love." Someone said to me the other day that he understood about belief, but he could not understand what it was to be born again. I told him that he that believed had life eternal, and whoever received life through Christ was born again. A man cannot get that life by merely going to church and observing forms; he must get the Spirit of God, and then he will have light and peace. We have no peace so long as we have sin, but if we accept Christ, and salvation through him, our sins are blotted out, and we have peace in reviewing the past.

Spiritual power is what we want next. As soon as the Holy Ghost comes we want boldness to go out and proclaim Jesus. There was once a man on trial for his life. The king of the country in which he lived said the law must take its course, but, after he was tried and condemned, he would pardon him. The man was cool all through his trial, and when they brought in a verdict of guilty, the man was perfectly unconcerned. So with the Christian. He will have boldness in his heart on the day of judgment, because he knows Christ became a propitiation for his sins and he has his pardon laid up in his heart.

One Thing Lacking

Here is a man who seems to be good enough without Christ. Cornelius, we are told, was devout, just, benevolent, of good report among all nations, and a man who feared God. What more could you ask? What did he lack? He needed Christ. I don't care how good a man may be, he needs a Savior.

We ought to be interested in this account of the conversion of Cornelius, for if he needed it, we all need it—every person in New York needs it. It is recorded that an angel of God appeared to Cornelius and told him to send to Joppa for Peter that he might come to his house and tell them words whereby they might be saved. And Cornelius sent three men and Peter returned with them to Caesarea. We all ought to want to know what the message was that the disciple brought. What was necessary for the salvation of so good a man is necessary for us all.

"God anointed Jesus of Nazareth with the Holy Ghost and with power, who went about doing good, and healing all that were oppressed of the devil, for God was with him." You may be everything that is estimable, but if you don't believe in Jesus Christ and receive remission of your sins, you cannot see heaven. Under that preaching of Peter's, Cornelius and his whole family were converted. The Holy Ghost fell upon the meeting, and it was a good net that the disciple drew in that day. Let us pray that we may receive the Spirit as they did.

Three Classes

I always notice many here at noon whom we have met in the inquiry rooms, and I want to speak a word to them. There are three classes of people who will not accept salvation—those who neglect it, those who refuse it, and those who despise it. Many think they are not so bad as the scoffer at religion because they only neglect it, but if they keep on in that path they are lost just the same. Suppose there is a man in a boat going in a swift current down the stream; if he neglects to pull for the shore he is a doomed man. He will go over the rapids won't he? If Noah had neglected to go into the ark after he had built it, he would have been lost with the other antediluvians. Nothing could have saved him. You let the cry be raised that this building is on fire, and see how many will keep their seats; they would be burned up as sure as they did.

Then again in the twelfth chapter of Hebrews, twenty-fifth verse, we read: "See that ye refuse not him that speaketh." The next step is to refuse salvation. A while ago they only neglected it, now they refuse it—that is the second rung of the ladder. You can only do one of two things, take it or refuse it. You have all been in a house where the waiter passed ice-water to a number of people sitting together, and seen how some would take it and some would not; so the cup of salvation is passed among you today. How many of you will accept it? Are you almost persuaded? Remember a hair's breadth from heaven is not an inch from hell.

Again in the tenth chapter of Hebrews, twenty-eighth verse, we read: "He that despised Moses' law died without mercy under two or three witnesses." Many despise the whole thing, hate it, and will have none of it—give them a tract and they light their cigars with it. There are the three words—neglect, refuse, despise. When there is but one engine and three cars attached, don't they all go the same way? If you do either of these three things, you must suffer the eternal consequences.

Prayers by Mr. Moody 12

I

Our Heavenly Father, we come to wait on thee for the gift of thy Spirit of service. We want it above everything else. O God, give us the Spirit! Empty us of self, of self-seeking. O God, bring us down into the dust before thee, so that we may be filled with the Holy Ghost, so that we may have power with God and with man! O thou God of Elijah, we pray that a double portion of thy Spirit may come upon us today, that we may be anointed to do the work thou hast for us to do! We know that we have but a little while to stay here. In a few months or years, at longest, we will all be gone. O God, help us to bear fruit while we live! May we no longer be living in this lukewarm state. May we no longer go toiling day after day and month after month, and seeing no fruit. O Jesus, Master, thou hast gone up on high; thou hast led captivity captive; thou art at the right hand of God, and thou hast power. O give us power! Thou canst impart power. Thou canst quicken us into new life. Thou canst give us a fresh anointing. We pray that thou will do it today. We pray that thou wilt breath upon us a breath from heaven. Grant that we may know what it is to have the Holy Ghost resting upon us for service. We pray for these ministers that are going to stand up in their pulpits on the coming Sabbath. O may there be a new man in every pulpit! May the power of God rest upon them and upon their ministry! Bless, we pray thee, the elders, the deacons, and the church officers, the stewards, and the wardens.

O God, breathe upon them the breath of life! And may there be a quickening in every gospel church. We ask it all in the name and for the sake of thy blessed Son. Amen.

II

Our Heavenly Father, help us now to realize that we are in thy presence. Help us to realize how holy and pure thou art, and how impure we are. We would take the place of the Publican today, and we would smite upon our breasts, and cry, "God be merciful to us sinners!" We are not worthy of thy love; we are not worthy of thy mercy, but Jesus has bid us come in his name, and make our wants known. O Blessed Heavenly Father, for Jesus Christ's sake, bless every soul in this hall today! We pray that there may not be one that shall leave this hall today with the spirit of the Pharisee! May we not go out of here thanking God that we are not like other people! Oh, may we take our place in the dust, and may our cry be, "God be merciful to me, a sinner!" Or may our cry be like that of the Syro-Phoenician woman, "Lord help me!" Or like that of Peter, "Lord, save or I perish!" If thou dost not save us, Blessed Master, we will perish, and so we come to thee for salvation. We come to thee for help today, and now we pray that thou wilt give us help. Amen.

III

Our Heavenly Father, we thank thee for the privilege we have this beautiful Sabbath day of coming together within these walls, to worship thee, and we pray that thou wilt give us today the Spirit, for we read in thy word that they that worship thee must worship thee in spirit and in truth; so we ask that thou wilt give us today freely of the Spirit that we may know how to approach thee; we may know how to come to thee with all our wants; that we may know how to make our requests known unto thee. And we pray that today, as we attempt to lift out thoughts to thee in prayer, thou wilt hear and answer our prayer and give us today a token of what we are to have in this city in this coming month. We pray that this may be the best month that this city has ever seen; that there may be days of the right hand power of the Son of God. We pray that there may be a blessed and mighty work of Christ in this city. All our expectations are from thee. We know that man has not the power to reach the human heart; but we pray that the Spirit may convict of sin, that the Holy Ghost may do his office work, and that the work may be deep and thorough; that it may not be the work of the flesh; that it may not be the work of man; that it may not be like the morning cloud that shall soon pass away; but may it be deep and thorough; may it be the work of God Almighty; and we pray that each one of us may take our places in the dust before thee, and that we may humble ourselves under thy hand, so that thou canst shine and speak through us, who bear the name of Jesus Christ.

May the day be not far distant when there shall be streams of salvation going forth from this city that shall make the towns and villages throughout this great state glad. We pray that there may be power in all these meetings, that the power of the Lord may be present to heal those that shall gather within those walls.

And we pray for the careless and indifferent that have come here this afternoon out of idle curiosity. Oh, that there may be power here today to convict them of sin and to convert them, that they may become children of God and heirs of heaven.

We pray for those who have gone to the other meeting. May the Spirit be there in mighty power, and may those that may speak, speak with power from on high, and may the power of God be not only upon the speakers, but upon him who shall sing the songs of Zion.

We pray that thou wilt bless the singing of these gospel hymns; and as our brother shall sing from day to day here, we pray that the Spirit may carry the truth down into the hearts of the people; that there may be many that shall be blessed by hearing the gospel sung.

Now, Heavenly Father, wilt thou give us all the spirit of prayer and supplication, and while we are here together today may there be one wave of united prayer going to the throne of grace, for the power of God to be felt here; and Christ shall have all the praise and glory. Amen.

IV

Our Heavenly Father, we look again to thee for thy blessing upon this waiting congregation. We pray that thou wilt this night help us as we wait upon thee. Help us to call our wandering thoughts in from the world, from its cares, from its troubles, and from its pleasures, and may our thoughts be centered upon heaven and heavenly things tonight, and may every heart in this assembly receive the word of God; may that word be preached with power, and may it find its way to many a heart; may very many have the moral courage given them to stand up and confess the Lord Jesus Christ in their homes or in their places of business, and wherever their lot may be cast. Lord, help each one of us that professes to be thy disciple to be bold and fearless. May we not be ashamed of the cross of Jesus Christ, which is the power of God unto salvation. Oh, may each and every one of us be ready at all times and in all places to confess him who loved us and gave himself for us. O God, we now look to thee for thy blessing upon those that have come in here out of mere curiosity. May the Spirit of God touch their heart's tonight. May the scales be removed from their eyes. May they believe the record of God's Son. May they believe on the Lord Jesus Christ and be saved. May this be the night of their salvation. May this be the night we have prayed for—the night when God shall make bare his arm to save. May there be a great salvation of souls tonight. We pray thy blessing to rest upon the men's meeting in yonder church. Son of God, go with us as we go from this building to that meeting. May there be many drawn to that place; may there be many that shall stand on the Lord's side, and we shall give Christ the praise and glory in this life and in the life to come. Amen.

V

Our Heavenly Father, we now look to thee for thy blessing upon the hymns that have been sung, and upon the word of God that shall be read, and the remarks that shall be made. We pray that the Spirit of God may be here tonight, carrying home the truth to our hearts and consciences, and may the blind eyes be opened that men may see Christ; that they may see their need of the blessed Savior that has come into the world to seek and to save that which was lost, for thou knowest how sin has blinded many and how Satan has deceived thousands, and how the world is luring men away from heaven and from eternity and from eternal things. O thou God of all grace, let thy power be felt here tonight. Give us, we pray thee, freely of the Spirit. May the Spirit of God do its office work, and may there be many that shall be led to inquire what they shall do to be saved tonight.

Bless our brother who shall preach the adjoining church tonight; let thy blessing rest upon him. May very many be born of the Spirit, born again, born from above, that we may meet them in thy kingdom. We ask it in the name and for the sake of thy beloved Son. Amen.

VI

Our Heavenly Father, we thank thee for thy blessing and precious word, for the privilege we have this evening of reading the words that fell from the lips of our God and Master while here upon earth. We pray that thou wilt teach us to understand the lesson that thou wouldst teach us by this miracle. Lord, help us that we may cast away all unbelief. We pray that there may be many in this city of Cleveland sitting at thy feet clothed and in their right minds with the evil spirit cast out of them. Son of God, manifest thy power in this place tonight. Make this place awfully solemn on account of thy power. Give us a message from on high. May the word sink deep into our hearts. May much good be done here this night. We pray that thy blessing may rest on each and every one of us that profess to be disciples of the Son of God. May we hunger and thirst until we are filled with righteousness, with faith and the Holy Ghost. We pray that thou wilt remember in much mercy the Christian workers gathered here tonight. May they have fresh power given them—a new life, a new power. We pray for all these church officers, for the deacons, the elders, the church wardens and stewards gathered here tonight. We pray for every Sabbath school superintendent and Sabbath school teacher. Give them to understand the worth of souls. May they awake to their great responsibilities resting upon us. Grant that during the next thirty days in this city we may see them coming by scores and by hundreds into thy kingdom, and thy name, blessed Savior, shall have the praise and glory. Amen.

VII

Our Heavenly Father, we pray that thy blessing may rest upon the words that have been spoken in weakness. May they be carried home to our hearts with power, and grant that there may be many a heart stirred here tonight to go out into the vineyard and work for thee. O Lord, help us parents to labor for the salvation of our children, that they may be with us in glory and not one of them shall be missing when thou comest to make up thy jewels. Wilt thou spare them as man spares his own son. May we have the joy of seeing them come in the morning of their lives and give themselves to thee.

And now we pray for those Sabbath school teachers. May their hearts be burdened this night for their scholars, and may they not rest, but may they go to their homes and may they plead with them to come to Christ. May they bring them to the meeting, and may we have the joy of seeing them coming out and taking their stand on the Lord's side. O Father! For Jesus Christ's sake wilt thou hear our prayer and wilt thou answer our petition; and grant that this night the answer may come. May we not rest day nor night until we see those that are about us brought to the kingdom of God, and thy name shall have the praise and the glory. Amen.

VIII

Our Heavenly Father, we praise thee for this blessed gospel that brings such news. We thank thee that thou didst send Jesus Christ into this world to save it. And we thank thee, blessed Savior, that thou didst leave that upper world, and that thou hast lit it up by thine own light; that thou now dost come and offer to dwell with us.

Oh, that men may be wise tonight! Oh, that they may make room in their hearts for Jesus Christ! Oh, that they may say now from the depths of their heart, "Lord Jesus, come and dwell with me!" May they invite him to their hearts and homes as Martha and Mary did at Bethany.

O Spirit of God! Wilt thou work mightily, and grant that many this night may be born again, born of the Spirit, born from above, that they may this night take Christ to be their way, their truth and their life, and thy name shall have the praise and glory. Amen.

IX

Our Heavenly Father, open our eyes tonight that we may know whether we are building on the Rock of Ages or not. If we are building on a sandy foundation, may our minds be opened tonight by the Spirit of God so that we may know, and that we may be led to build upon that rock that thou hast laid in Zion, that precious corner stone, that tried stone, the stone that has been rejected by the builders, that has become the head and the corner stone. May we build all our hope upon that rock and that alone. Amen.

Heaven: Its Hope 13

COLOSSIANS 1:3-5

We give thanks to God and the Father of our Lord Jesus Christ, praying always for you, Since we heard of your faith in Christ Jesus, and of the love which ye have to all the saints, For the hope which is laid up for you in heaven, whereof ye heard before in the word of the truth of the gospel.

A great many persons imagine that anything said about heaven is only a matter of speculation. They talk about heaven much as they would about the air. Now there would not have been so much in Scripture on this subject if God had wanted to leave the human race in darkness about it. "All Scripture," we are told, "is given by inspiration of God, and is profitable for doctrine, for reproof, for correction, for instruction in righteousness; that the man of God may be perfect, thoroughly furnished unto all good works."

What the Bible says about heaven is just as true as what it says about everything else. The Bible is inspired. What we are taught about heaven could not have come to us in any other way but by inspiration. No one knew anything about it but God; and so if we want to find out anything about it, we have to turn to his word. Dr. Hodge, of Princeton, says that the best evidence of the Bible being the word of God is to be found between its own two covers. It proves itself. In this respect it is like Christ, whose character proclaimed the divinity of his person. Christ showed himself more than man by what he did. The Bible shows itself more than a human book by what it says.

It seems perfectly reasonable that in the Bible God should have given us a glimpse of the future, for we are constantly losing some of our friends by death, and the first thought that comes to us is, "Where have they gone?" When a loved one is taken away from us, how that thought comes up before us! How we wonder if we shall ever see him or her again, and where and when it will be! Then it is that we turn to this blessed Book; for there is no other book in all the world that can give us the slightest comfort—no other book that can tell us where the loved ones have gone.

Not long ago I met an old friend, and as I took him by the hand and asked after his family, the tears came trickling down his cheeks as he said: "I haven't any now." "What!" I said, "is your wife dead?" "Yes, sir."

"And all your children too?" "Yes, all gone!" he said; "and I am left here desolate and alone." Would anyone take from that man the hope that he will meet his dear ones again? Would anyone persuade him that there is not a future where the lost will be found? No, we need not forget our dear loved ones; but we may cling for ever to the enduring hope that there will be a time when we can meet unfettered, and be blest in that land of everlasting suns, where the soul drinks from the living streams of love that roll by God's high throne.

There are those who say that there is no heaven. I was once talking with a man who said he thought there was nothing to justify us in believing in any other heaven than we know here on earth. If this is heaven, it is a very strange one—this world of sickness, and sorrow, and sin. I pity from the depths of my heart the man or woman who has that idea.

This world, that some think is heaven, is the home of sin, a hospital of sorrow, a place that has nothing in it to satisfy the soul. Men go all over it, and then want to get out of it. The more men see of the world the less they think of it. People soon grow tired of the best pleasures it has to offer. Someone has said that the world is a stormy sea, whose every wave is strewn with the wrecks of mortals that perish in it. Every time we breathe someone is dying. We all know that we are going to stay here but a very little while. Our life is but a vapor. It is just a mere shadow.

I do not think that it is wrong for us to think and talk about heaven. I like to locate heaven, and find out all I can about it. I expect to live there through all eternity. If I were going to dwell in any place in this country, if I were going to make it my home, I should want to inquire about the place, about its climate, about the neighbors I should have, and about everything in fact that I could learn concerning it. If any of you were going to emigrate, that would be the way you would feel.

Well, we are all going to emigrate in a very little while to a country that is very far away. We are going to spend eternity in another world, a grand and glorious world where God reigns. Is it not natural then, that we should look, and listen, and try to find out who is already there, and what is the route to take?

Soon after I was converted, an infidel asked me one day why I looked *up* when I prayed. He said that heaven was no more above us than below us; that heaven was everywhere. Well, I was greatly bewildered, and the next time I prayed, it seemed almost as if I was praying into the air. Since then I have become better acquainted with the Bible, and I have come to see that heaven is above us; that it is upward, and not downward. The Spirit of God is everywhere; but God is in heaven, and heaven is above our heads. It does not matter what part of the globe we may stand upon, heaven is above us.

In Genesis 17 we read that God *went up* to heaven and in John 3 we read that the Son of Man came *down* from heaven. So, in Acts 1, we find that Christ went *up* into heaven and a cloud received him out of sight. Thus we can see that heaven is up. The very arrangement of the firmament about the earth declares the seat of God's glory to be above us. Job says, "Let not God regard it from *above*."

Again, in Deuteronomy, we read, "Who shall go *up* for us to heaven?"

Thus, all through Scripture we find that we are given the location of heaven as upward, and beyond the firmament. This firmament, with its many bright worlds, is so vast that heaven must be an extensive realm. Yet this need not surprise us. It is not for us to inquire why God made heaven so extensive that its lights along the way can be seen from any place on this little world.

In Jeremiah 51:15 we are told that "He hath made the earth by his power; he hath established the world by his wisdom, and hath stretched out the heaven by his understanding." Yet how little we really know of that power, or wisdom, or understanding! As we read in Job 26:14, "Lo, these are parts of his ways: but how little a portion is heard of him! But the thunder of his power who can understand?" or as we find it in Isaiah 42:5, "Thus saith God the Lord, he that created the heavens and stretched them out; he that spread forth the earth, and that which cometh out of it; he that giveth bread unto the people upon it, and Spirit to them that walk therein."

The discernment of God's power, the messages of heaven, do not always come in great things. As we read in 1 Kings 19:11–12, "And behold, the Lord passed by, and a great and strong wind rent the mountains, and brake in pieces the rocks before the Lord, but the Lord was not in the wind; and after the wind an earthquake, but the Lord was not in the earthquake; and after the earthquake a fire, but the Lord was not in the fire; and after the fire a still small voice." It is as a "still small voice" that God speaks to his children.

Some people are trying to find out just how far heaven is away. There is one thing we know about it; that is, that it is not so far away but that God can hear us when we pray. I do not believe there has ever been a tear shed for sin since Adam's fall in Eden to the present time, but God has witnessed it. He is not too far from this earth for us to go to him; and if there is a sigh that comes from a burdened heart today, God will hear that sigh. If there is a cry coming up from a heart broken on account of sin, God will hear that cry. He is not so far away—heaven is not so far away—as to be inaccessible to the smallest child. In 2 Chronicles 7:14, we read, "If my people, which are called by my name, shall humble themselves, and pray, and seek my face, and turn from their wicked ways; then will I hear from heaven, and will forgive their sin, and will heal their land."

When I was in Dublin, they were telling me about a father who had lost a little boy. This father had not thought about the future, he had been so entirely taken up with this world and its affairs; but when that little boy, his only child, died, the father's heart was broken; and every night when he got home from work, he was found in his room with his candle and his Bible, hunting up all that he could find there about heaven. Someone asked him what he was doing, and he said he was trying to find out where his child had gone; and I think he was a reasonable man. I suppose there is not a man or woman but has dear ones who are departed. Shall we close this Book today? Or shall we look into it to try to find where the loved ones are?

I was reading, some time ago, an account of a father, a minister, who had lost a child. He had gone to a great many funerals, offering comfort to others in sorrow; but now the iron had entered his own soul, and a brother minister had come to officiate and preach the funeral sermon. After this minister had finished speaking, the father got up, and standing at the head of the coffin, he said that a few years ago, when he had first come into that parish, as he used to look over the river he took no interest in the people over there, because they were all strangers to him, and there were none over there that belonged to his parish. But, he said, a few years ago a young man came into his home, and married his daughter, and she went over the river to live; and when his child went over there, he became suddenly interested in the inhabitants, and every morning as he arose he looked out of the window across the river to her home. "But now," he said, "another child has been taken. She has gone over another river; and heaven seems dearer and nearer to me now than it ever has been before."

My friends, let us believe this good old Book; be confident that heaven is not a myth; and let us be prepared to follow the dear ones who have gone before. Thus, and thus alone, can we find the peace we seek for.

Seeking a Better Country

What has been, and is now, one of the strongest feelings in the human heart? Is it not to find some better place, some lovelier spot, than we have now? It is for this that men are seeking everywhere. And they can have it, if they will; but instead of looking down, they must look up to find it. As men grow in knowledge, they vie with each other more and more in making their homes attractive; but the brightest home on earth is but an empty barn, compared with the mansions that are in the skies.

What is it that we look for at the decline and close of life? Is it not some sheltered place, some quiet spot, where if we cannot have constant rest, we may at least have a foretaste of the rest that is to be. What was it that led Columbus, not knowing what would be his fate, across the unsailed western seas, if it were not the hope of finding a better country? This it was that sustained the hearts of the Pilgrim fathers, driven from their native land by persecution, as they faced an iron-bound, savage coast, with an unexplored territory beyond. They were cheered and upheld by the hope of reaching a free and fruitful country, where they could be at rest and worship God in peace.

Somewhat similar is the Christian's hope of heaven; only it is not an undiscovered country, and in attractions it cannot be compared with anything we know on earth. Perhaps nothing but the shortness of our range of sight keeps us from seeing the celestial gates all open to us; and perhaps nothing but the deafness of our ears prevents our hearing the joyful ringing of the bells of heaven. There are constant sounds around us that we cannot hear; and the sky is studded with bright worlds that our eyes have never seen. Little as we know about this bright and radiant land, there are glimpses of its beauty that come to us now and then.

We may not know how sweet its balmy air,
How bright and fair its flowers;
We may not hear the songs that echo there,
Through these enchanted bowers.

The city's shining towers we may not see
With our dim earthly vision;
For death, the silent warder, keeps the key
That opes the gates elysian.

But sometimes when adown the western sky
A fiery sunset lingers,
Its golden gates swing inward noiselessly,
Unlocked by unseen fingers.

And while they stand a moment half-ajar,
Gleams from the inner glory
Stream brightly through the azure vault afar,
And half reveal the story.

It is said by travelers, that in climbing the Alps the houses of far distant villages can be seen with great distinctness, so that sometimes the number of panes of glass in a church window can be counted. The distance looks so short that the place whither the traveler is journeying appears almost at hand; but after hours and hours of climbing, seems no nearer yet. This is because of the clearness of the atmosphere. By perseverance, however, the goal is reached at last, and the tired traveler finds rest. So sometimes we dwell in high altitudes of grace; heaven seems very near, and the hills of Beulah are in full view. At other times the clouds and fogs caused by suffering and sin cut off our sight. We are just as near heaven in the one case as we are in the other; and we are just as sure of gaining it if we only keep in the path that Christ has trod.

I have read that on the shores of the Adriatic Sea, the wives of fishermen, whose husbands have gone far out upon the deep, are in the habit of going down to the sea-shore at night and singing with their sweet voices the first verse of some beautiful hymn. After they have sung it they listen until they hear brought on the wind, across the sea, the second verse sung by their brave husbands as they are tossed by the waves—and both are happy. Perhaps, if we would listen, we too might hear on this sea-tossed world of ours, some sound, some whisper, borne from afar to tell us there is a heaven which is our home; and when we sing our hymns upon the shores of earth, perhaps we may hear their sweet echoes breaking in music upon the sands of time, and cheering the hearts of those who are pilgrims and strangers along the way. Yes, we need to look up—out, beyond this low earth, and to build higher in our thoughts and actions, even here!

You know, when a man is going up in a balloon, he takes in sand as ballast, and when he wants to mount a little higher, he throws out some of the ballast, and then he mounts higher; he throws out more ballast, and he mounts still higher. And the more sand he throws out the higher he gets: so the nearer we would get to God the more we have to throw out of the things of this world. Let go of them; do not let us set our hearts and affections on them, but do what the Master tells us—lay up for ourselves treasure in heaven.

In England I was told of a lady who had been bedridden for years. She was one of those saints that God polishes up for the kingdom; for I believe that there are a good many saints in this world that we never hear about; we never see their names heralded through the press; they live very near the Master; and they live very near heaven. I think it takes a great deal more grace to suffer God's will than it does to do God's will. And if a person lies on a bed of sickness, and suffers cheerfully, it is just as acceptable to God as if such a one went out and worked in his vineyard. Now, this lady was one of those saints. She said that for a long time she used to have a great deal of pleasure in watching a bird that came to make its nest near her window. One year it came to make its nest, and it began to make it so low down that the lady was afraid something would happen to the young ones; and everyday that she saw that bird busy at work making its nest, she kept saying, "O bird, build higher!" She could see that the bird was likely to come to grief and disappointment. At last the bird finished her nest, and laid eggs, and hatched her young. Every morning the lady looked out to see if the nest was still there: she saw the old bird bringing food for the little ones, and she took a great deal of pleasure in watching them. But one morning, when she woke up and looked out, she saw nothing but feathers scattered all around, and she said, "Ah, the cat has got the old bird and all her young!"

It would have been a kindness to have torn that nest down. That is what God does for us very often—just snatches things away before it is too late. Now, I think that is what we want to say to professing Christians—that if you build for time you will be disappointed. God says: Build up yonder! It is a good deal better to have life with Christ in God than anywhere else. I would rather have my life hid with Christ in God than be in Eden as Adam was. Adam might have remained in Paradise for sixteen thousand years, and then have fallen; but if our life is hid in Christ, how safe!

Heaven: Its Inhabitants

14

ISAIAH 33:24

And the inhabitant shall not say, I am sick: the people that dwell therein shall be forgiven their iniquity.

The society of heaven will be select. No one who studies Scripture can doubt that. There are a good many kinds of aristocracy in this world; but the aristocracy of heaven will be the aristocracy of holiness. The humblest believer on earth will be an aristocrat there. We read in Isaiah 57: "Thus saith the High and Lofty One, that inhabiteth eternity, whose name is Holy: I dwell in the high and holy place, with him also that is of a contrite and humble spirit." Now what could be plainer than that? No one who is not of a contrite and humble spirit will dwell with God in his high and holy place.

If there is anything that ought to make heaven dear to Christians, it is knowing that God and all their loved ones will be there. What is it that makes home so attractive? Is it because we have a beautiful home? Is it because we have beautiful lawns? Is it because we have beautiful trees around us? Is it because we have beautiful paintings upon the walls inside? Is it because we have beautiful furniture? Is that all that makes home so attractive and so beautiful? Nay, it is the loved ones within it; it is the loved ones there.

I remember, after being away from home some time, I went back to see my honored mother. I thought that in going back I would take her by surprise, and steal in unexpectedly upon her; but when I found she had gone away, the old place did not seem like home at all. I went into one room, and then into another, and then all through the house, but I could not find that loved mother; and I inquired of some member of the family, "Where is mother?" and they said she had gone away. Well, home had lost its charm to me; it was that mother that made home so sweet to me, and it is the loved ones that make home so sweet to everyone. It is the presence of the loved ones that will make heaven so sweet to all of us. Christ is there; God the Father is there; and many, many who were dear to us when they lived on earth are there—and we shall be with them by and by.

We find clearly in Matthew 18:10 that the angels are also there: "Take heed that ye despise not one of these little ones; for I say unto you, that in heaven their angels do always behold the face of my Father which is in heaven." Their angels do always behold the Father's face! We shall have good company up there—not only those who have been redeemed, but those who have never been lost; those who have never known what it is to transgress; those who have never known what it is to be disobedient; those who have obeyed him from the very morning of creation.

It has been said that there will be three things which will surprise us when we get to heaven: one, to find many there whom we did not expect to find there; another, to find some not there whom we had expected; and a third, and perhaps the greatest wonder, will be to find ourselves there.

A poor woman once told Rowland Hill that the way to heaven was short, easy, and simple, comprising only three steps—out of self, into Christ, and into glory. We have a shorter way now—out of self and into Christ, and we are there. As a dead man cannot inherit an estate, no more can a dead soul inherit heaven. The soul must be raised up in Christ. Among the good whom we hope to meet in heaven, we are told, there will be every variety of character, taste, and disposition. There is not one mansion there; there are *many*. There is not one gate to heaven, but *many*. There are not only three gates on the north, but on the east three gates, and on the west three gates, and on the south three gates. From opposite quarters of the theological compass, from opposite quarters of the religious world, from opposite quarters of human life and character, through different expressions of their common faith and hope, through different modes of conversion, through different portions of the Holy Scripture, will the weary travelers enter the Heavenly City, and meet each other—"not without surprise"—on the shores of the river of life. And on those shores they will find a tree bearing, not the same kind of fruit always and at all times, but "twelve manner of fruits," for every different turn of mind—for the patient sufferer, for the active servant, for the holy and humble philosopher, for the spirits of just men now at last made perfect. And "the leaves of the tree shall be for the healing," not of one single church or people only, not for the Scotsman or the Englishman only, but for the "healing of the nations"—the Frenchman, the German, the Italian, the Russian—for all those from whom, it may be, in this, its fruits have been farthest removed, but who, nevertheless, have "hungered and thirsted after righteousness," and who therefore "shall be filled."

An eminent living divine once commented: "When I was a boy, I thought of heaven as a great, shining city, with vast walls and domes and spires, and with nobody in it except white-robed angels, who were strangers to me. By and by my little brother died; and I thought of a great city with walls and domes and spires, and a flock of cold, unknown angels, and one little fellow that I was acquainted with. He was the only one I knew at that time. Then another brother died, and there were two that I knew. Then my acquaintances began to die, and the flock continually grew. But it was not till I had sent one of my little children to his Heavenly Parent—God—that I began to think I had got a little in myself. A second went; a third went; a fourth went; and by that time I had so many acquaintances in heaven, that I no longer thought of the walls and domes and spires. I began to think of the residents of the celestial city. And now so many of my acquaintances have gone there, that it sometimes seems to me that I know more in heaven than I do on earth."

We Shall Live Forever

We read in John 12:26: "If any man serve me, let him follow me; and where I am, there shall also my servant be." I cannot agree with some people, that Paul has been sleeping in the grave, and is still there, after the storms of eighteen hundred years. I cannot believe that he who loved the Master, who had such a burning zeal for him, has been separated from him in an unconscious state.

Now when a man believes on the Lord Jesus Christ, he gets eternal life. A great many people make a mistake just there. "He that believeth on the Son hath—*h-a-t-h*—hath eternal life"; it is not said that he shall have it when he comes to die; the word is in the present tense; it is mine now—if I believe. He is the "gift of God." That is enough. You cannot bury the gift of God; you cannot bury eternal life. All the gravediggers in the world cannot bury eternal life. All the gravediggers in the world cannot dig a grave large enough and deep enough to hold eternal life; all the coffin-makers of the world cannot make a coffin large enough and deep enough to hold eternal life: It is mine! It is mine!

I believe when Paul said, "absent from the body, present with the Lord," he meant what he said; that he was not going to be separated from him for eighteen hundred years; that Spirit that he received when he was converted he had from a new life and a new nature, and they could not lay that away in the sepulchre; they could not bury that; that flew to meet its Maker. It may be he is not fully satisfied, and will not be until the resurrection, for Christ says: "He shall see of the travail of his soul, and shall be satisfied" (Isaiah 53:11). Even the body shall be raised; this body, sown in dishonor, shall be raised in glory; this body, which has known corruption, shall put on incorruption; and this mortal shall put on immortality. It is only a question of time. The great morning of the world will, by-and-by, dawn upon the earth, and the dead shall come forth and shall hear the voice of him who is the resurrection and the life.

Paul wrote: "If our earthly house of this tabernacle were dissolved, we have a building of God, an house not made with hands, eternal in the heavens." He could take down the clay temple, and leave that; but he had a better house. "I am in a strait betwixt two, having a desire to depart, and to be with Christ; which is far better: nevertheless to abide in the flesh is more needful for you." To me it is a sweet thought that death does not separate us from the Master. A great many people are living continually in the bondage of death; but if I have eternal life, death cannot touch that; it may touch the house I live in; it may change my countenance and send my body away to the grave; but it cannot touch this new life.

To me it is very sad to think that so many professed Christians look upon death as they do. I received some time ago a letter from a friend in London; and I thought, as I read it, I would take and show it to other people and see if I could not get them to look upon death as this friend did. He had lost a loved mother. In England it is a very common thing to send out cards in memory of the departed ones. They put upon them great borders of black—sometimes a quarter of an inch of black border; but this friend had put on a gold border, since his mother had gone to the golden city.

It is not death at all; it is life. Someone said to a person dying: "Well, you are in the land of the living yet." "No," said he, "I am in the land of the dying yet; but I am going to the land of the living: they live there, and never die." This is the land of sin and death and tears, but up yonder they never die. It is perpetual life; it is unceasing joy.

"It is a glorious thing to die," was the testimony of Hannah More on her deathbed, though her life had been sown thick with the rarest friendships, and age had not so weakened her memory as to cause her to forget those little hamlets among the cliffs of her native hills, or the mission schools she had with such perseverance established, and where she would be so sadly missed.

James Montgomery has said:

There is a soft, a downy bed;
'Tis fair as breath of even;
A couch for weary mortals spread,
Where they may rest the aching head,
And find repose—in heaven!

There is an hour of peaceful rest,
To mourning wanderers given;
There is a joy for souls distressed,
A balm for every wounded breast—
'Tis found alone—in heaven!

Will We Know Our Friends in Heaven?

Many are anxious to know if they will recognize their friends in heaven. In Matthew 8:11, we read, "I say unto you, that many shall come from the east and west, and shall sit down with Abraham, and Isaac, and Jacob, in the kingdom of heaven." Here we find that Abraham, who lived so many hundreds of years before Christ, had not lost his identity; and Christ tells us that the time is coming when many shall come from the east and west and shall sit down with Abraham and Isaac and Jacob in the kingdom of God. These men had not lost their identity; they were known as Abraham, Isaac, and Jacob. And if you will turn to that wonderful scene that took place on the Mount of Transfiguration, you will find that Moses, who had been gone from the earth fifteen hundred years, was there; Peter, James, and John saw him on the Mount of Transfiguration; they saw him as Moses; he had not lost his name. Christ says of him that overcometh, "I will not blot out his name out of the Book of Life." We have names in heaven; we are going to bear our names there; we shall be known.

In Psalm 17:15 it says: "When I awake with thy likeness I shall be satisfied." That is enough. "Want" is written on every human heart down here; but there we shall be satisfied. You may hunt the world from one end to the other, and you will not find a man or woman who is satisfied; but in heaven we shall want for nothing. In 1 John 3, speaking to the followers of Christ, the Apostle says, "Beloved, now are we the sons of God, and it doth not yet appear what we shall be; but we know that when he shall appear, we shall be like him; for we shall see him as he is. And every man that hath this hope in him purifieth himself, even as he is pure."

Moreover, it seems highly probable—indeed I think it is clearly taught by Scripture—that a great many careless Christians will get into heaven. There will be a great many who will get in by the skin of their teeth, or as Lot was saved from Sodom, "so as by fire." They will barely get in, but there will be no crown of rejoicing. But *everybody* is not going to rush into heaven. There are a great many who *will not* be there. You know we have a class of people who tell us they are going into the kingdom of God, whether they are converted or not. They tell us that they are on their way; that they are going there. They tell us all are going there; that good, bad, and indifferent are all going into the kingdom, and that they will all be there; that there is no difference;

and, in other words—if I may be allowed to use plain language—they give God the lie.

But they say, "We believe in the *mercy* of God." So do I. I believe in the *justice* of God, too; and I think heaven would be a good deal worse than this earth if unrenewed men were permitted to form part of it. Why, if a man should live for ever in this world in sin, what would become of this world? It seems as if it would be *hell itself*. Let your mind pass over the history of this country, and think of some who have lived in it. Suppose they never should die; suppose they should live on and on for ever in sin and rebellion. Do you think that God is going to take those who have rejected his Son, who have rejected the offer of his mercy, who have rejected salvation, and have just trampled his law under their feet, and have been in rebellion against his laws down here? Do you suppose God is going to take them right into his kingdom and let them live there for ever? By no means!

Some Will Not Get In

In the days of Noah we read that he waded as it were through the Deluge. He was the only righteous man. But, according to the theory of some people, the rest of those men who were so foul and so wicked—too wicked to live—God just took and swept them all into heaven, and left the only righteous man to go through this trial. Drunkards, and thieves, and vagabonds, all went to heaven, they say. You might as well go forward and preach: "You can swear as much as you like, and murder as much as you please, and it will all come out right—God will forgive you; God is so merciful."

Suppose the governor of a state should pardon every person that the courts ever convicted, all who are now lying in its jails and penitentiaries; suppose he should let them all loose because he is so merciful that he could not bear to have men punished; I think he would not be governor of that state long. Those men who are talking about God being so full of mercy, that he is going to spare and take all men to heaven, would be the very men to say that such a governor as that ought to be impeached, that he ought not to be governor. Let us bear in mind that the Scripture says there is a certain class of people who "shall not inherit the kingdom of God." Now, I will give you the Scripture; it is a good deal better to just give the Scripture for these things, and then if you do not like it you can quarrel with Scripture, and not with me. Let no man say that I have been saying who is going to heaven and who is not. I will let the Scripture speak for itself: "Know ye not that the unrighteous shall not inherit the kingdom of God?" (1 Corinthians 6:9). But "the unrighteous"—the adulterers, the fornicators, and thieves—these men may all inherit it, if they will only turn away from their sins. "Let the wicked forsake his way, and the unrighteous man his thoughts"; but if the unrighteous man says: "I will not turn away from sin; I will hold on to sin, and have heaven," he is deceiving himself.

A man who steals my pocketbook loses a good deal more than I do. I can afford to let him have my pocketbook a great deal better than he can afford to take it. See how much that man who steals my pocketbook loses. Perhaps he may get a few dollars; but he does not get much. See how much he has lost. Take an inventory of what that man loses if he loses heaven. Think of it! "No thief shall inherit the kingdom of God." To any thief I would say: "Steal no more." Let him ask God to forgive him; let him repent of his sin and turn to God. If you get eternal life it is worth more than the whole world. If you were to steal the whole world, you would not get much after all. The whole world does not amount to much, if with it you do not also have eternal life.

Heaven: Its Rewards 

1 CORINTHIANS 3:8

Now he that planteth and he that watereth are one: and every man shall receive his own reward according to his own labour.

If I understand things correctly, whenever you find men or women who are looking to be rewarded here for doing right, they are unqualified to work for God. If they are looking for the applause of men, looking for their reward in this life, it will disqualify them for the service of God, for they are all the while compromising truth.

They are afraid of hurting someone's feelings. They are afraid that someone is going to say something against them, or that there will be some newspaper articles written against them. Now, we must trample the world under our feet if we hope to get our reward hereafter. If we live for God we must suffer persecution. The kingdom of darkness and the kingdom of light are at war, and have been, and will be as long as Satan is permitted to reign in this world. As long as the kingdom of darkness is permitted to exist, there will be conflict; and if you want to be popular in the kingdom of God; if you want to be popular in heaven, and get a reward that shall last for ever—you will have to be unpopular here.

If you seek the applause of men, you cannot have the Lord say, "Well done!" at the end of the journey. You cannot have both. Why? Because this world is at war with God. This idea that the world is getting better is false. The old natural heart is just as much at enmity with God as it was when Cain slew Abel. Sin leaped into the world full grown in Cain. And from the time that Cain was born into the world to the present, man by nature has been at war with God.

On earth, we have to fight "the world, the flesh, and the devil." If we fight the world, the world will not like us. If we fight the flesh, the flesh will not like us. But by and by, we shall have our reward; and what a glorious reward it will be.

"Jesus said unto them, Ye are they which justify yourselves before men; but God knoweth your hearts: for that which is highly esteemed among men is abomination in the sight of God." We must go against the current of this world. If the world has nothing to say against us, we can be pretty sure that the Lord Jesus Christ has very little to say for us. There are those who do not like to go against the current of the world. They say they know this and that is wrong; but they do not say a word against it lest it might make them unpopular. If we expect to get the reward we must fight the good fight of faith. For all such, as Paul has said, "there is laid up a crown of righteousness, which the Lord, the righteous Judge, shall give us at that day" (2 Timothy 4:8).

The Fear of Death

How little we realize the meaning of the word eternity! The whole time between the creation of the world and the ending of it would not make a day in eternity. In time, it is like the infinity of space, whose center is everywhere and whose boundary is nowhere. As we read in the Epistle to the Hebrews: "Forasmuch then as the children are partakers of flesh and blood, he also himself likewise took part of the same; that through death he might destroy him that had the power of death—that is, the devil deliver them who through fear of death were all their lifetime subject to bondage."

There are a great many of God's professed children who live in continual bondage, in the constant fear of death. I believe this is dishonoring to God. I believe that it is not his will to have one of his children live in fear for one moment. If you know the truth in Jesus, there need be no fear, there need be no dread, because death will only hasten you on to glory; and your names are already written in heaven. And it is not only our privilege to have our names written in heaven, but also those of the children whom God has given us. The promise is not only to us, but to our children. Many a father's and many a mother's heart is burdened with anxiety for the salvation of their children. If your own name is there, let your next aim in life be to get the children that God has given you there also.

A mother was dying in one of our eastern cities a few years ago, leaving a large family of children. She was fading away in consumption; and the children were brought in to her one by one as she was sinking. She gave the eldest one her last message and her dying blessing; and then the next one was brought in; and the next; until at last they came to the little infant. She took it to her bosom and pressed it to her loving heart; her friends saw that it was hastening her end, that she was becoming excited; and they quickly took the little child from her. She said: "My husband, I charge you to bring all these children home with you!" And so God charges us, as parents, to bring our children home with us; not only to have our own names written in heaven, but those of our children also.

An eminent Christian worker in New York told me a story that affected me very much. A father had a son who had been sick some time; but he did not consider the lad's state dangerous, until one day he came home to dinner and found his wife weeping. He asked, "What is the trouble?" "There has been a great change in our boy since morning," the mother said, "and I am afraid that he is dying. I wish you would go in and see him; and, if you think he is dying, I wish you to tell him so, for I cannot bear to tell him."

The father went in and sat down by the bedside, and as he placed his hand upon his boy's forehead he could feel the cold, damp sweat of death, and knew its cold, icy hand was feeling for the chords of life, and that his boy was soon to be taken away. He said to him: "My son, do you know you are dying?" The little fellow looked up at him and said: "No! am I? Is this death that I feel stealing over me, father?" "Yes, my son, you are dying." "Shall I live the day out?" he asked. "No; you may die at any moment." He looked up to his father and he said: "Well, I shall be with Jesus tonight, shall I not, father?" And the father answered, "Yes, my boy, you will spend tonight with the Savior." And the father turned away to conceal his tears, that the little boy might not see him weep; but the son saw the tears, and he said, "Father, don't you weep for me. When I get to heaven I will go straight to Jesus and tell him that ever since I can remember you have tried to lead me to him."

I have three children, and the greatest desire of my heart is that they may be saved; that I may know that their names are written in the Book of Life. I may be taken from them early; I may leave them in this changing world without a father's care; but I would rather have them say of me after I am gone what that boy said of his father; or if they die before me, I would rather they should take that message to the Master—that ever since they can remember I have tried to lead them to the Savior—than have a monument over me reaching to the skies.

The roll is being called, and one after another summoned away; but if the names of our loved ones are registered in heaven, if we know that they are saved, and there—how sweet it is, after they have left us, to think that we shall meet them by and by; that we shall see them in the morn when the night has worn away.

During the late war a young man lay in a cot; and he was heard to say, "Here! Here!" Someone went to his cot and wanted to know what he wanted, and he said, "Hark! Hush! Don't you hear them?" "Hear whom?" he was asked. "They are calling the roll of heaven," he said. Soon afterward he answered, "Here!"—and he was gone.

If our names are in the Book of Life, by and by when the name is called, we shall say, like Samuel, "Here am I," and haste away to meet him. And if our children are called away early, oh it is so sweet to think that they died in Christ; that the great Shepherd gathers them in his arms and carries them in his bosom; and that we shall meet them by-and-by.

The Way to Heaven

The way to get to heaven is to be saved through faith in Jesus Christ. We get salvation as a gift; but we have to work it out, just as if we had *a gold mine* for a gift. I do not get a crown by joining a church, or renting a pew.

There was the Apostle Paul. He obtained his crown. He had many a hard fight; he met Satan on a good many battlefields, and he overcame him and wore the crown. It would take about ten thousand of the average Christians of this day to make one Paul. When I read the life of that Apostle, I blush for the Christianity of the nineteenth century. It is a weak and sickly thing.

See what he went through. Five times he was scourged. The old Roman custom of scourging was to take the prisoner and bind his wrists together and bend him over in a stooping posture, and the Roman soldier would bring down upon the bare back of the prisoner a lash formed of sharp pieces of steel, braided together; the lash cut through the skin, and men sometimes died in the very act of being scourged. Paul says, he was scourged five different times. Now if we should get one stripe upon our backs what a whining there would be! There would be forty publishers after us before the sun went down; and they would want to publish our story, that they might make capital out of it. But Paul says, "Five times received I forty stripes save one." That was nothing for him. Take your stand by his side.

"Paul, you have been beaten by these Jews four times; and they are going to give you thirty-nine stripes more. What are you going to do after you get out of the trouble? What are you going to do about it all?" "Do! Do!" he says; "I will do this one thing; I will press toward the mark for the prize of my high calling: I am on my way to get my crown." He was not going to lose his crown. "Don't think that a few stripes will turn me away: these light afflictions are nothing." And so they put on thirty-nine more stripes.

He had sprung into the race for Christ, as it were, and was leaping towards heaven. If you will allow me the expression—the devil got his match when he met Paul. He never switched off to a side-track. "This one thing I do," he said; "I am not going to lose the crown." See that no man takes your crown!

"Now, Paul, they have beaten you twice, and they are going to beat you again. What are you going to do? Are you going to continue preaching? If you are, let me give you a little advice. Don't be quite so radical. Be a little more conservative. Use a little finer language, and—so to speak—cover up the cross with beautiful words and flowery sentences. Tell men that they are pretty good after all—that they are not so bad. Get in with the world, and the world will think more of you. Don't be so earnest. Here's our advice. Now, what are you going to do?" "Do!" he responds; "I do this one thing—I press toward the mark for the prize of my high calling." So they lay on the rods, and every blow lifts him nearer to God.

"Now, Paul, we persist, this is growing serious. Had you not better take back some of the things you have said about Jesus? What are you going to do?" "Do!" he says; "If they take my life, I shall only get the crown the sooner." He would not budge an inch. He had something that the world could not give. He had something it could not take away. He had eternal life. He had waiting for him a crown of glory.

Thrice Paul suffered shipwreck; a day and a night was he in the deep. Look at that mighty apostle, a whole day and night in the deep. Shipwrecked. And for what? Was it to make money? He was not after money. He was just going from city to city, and town to town, to preach the glorious gospel of Jesus Christ, and to lift up the cross wherever he had the opportunity. He went down to Corinth, and preached there for eighteen months. None of the leaders of the Corinthian society came on the platform to sit by his side when he preached. There was not a man that stood by him. Down in Corinth, he did not have the leading businessmen advise him. The little tentmaker arrived in Corinth a perfect stranger; and the first thing he did was to find a place where he could make a tent. He did not go to a hotel. He earned his bread by the sweat of his brow. Think of that great apostle making a tent, and then going out to the corner of a street and preaching.

When I read of the life of such a man, how I blush to think how sickly and dwarfed Christianity is at the present time, and how many hundreds there are who never think of working for the Son of God, or of honoring Christ!

Yet when he wrote that letter back to Corinth, we find him taking an inventory of some things he had. He is rich, he says, "in journeyings often; in perils of waters; in perils by mine own countrymen; in perils by the heathen; in perils in the city; in perils in the wilderness; in perils in the sea; in perils amongst false brethren." That last must have been the hardest of all. "In weariness and painfulness; in watchings often; in hunger and thirst; in fastings often; in cold and nakedness." And besides all these, "the care of all the churches." And these are only some of the things that he summed up.

Do you know what made him so exceedingly glad? It was because he believed the Scripture; he believed that Sermon on the Mount. We profess to believe it; we pretend to believe it; but few of us more than half believe it. Listen to one sentence in that sermon: "Rejoice and be exceeding glad; for great is your reward in heaven" when you are persecuted. Now persecution was about all that Paul had. This was his capital, and he had a good deal of it: he had laid by a good many persecutions, and he was to get a great reward.

Christ says, "Rejoice and be exceeding glad, for great is your reward in heaven." If Jesus Christ spoke of it as "great," the reward must be wonderful indeed. We call things "great" that may look very small to Jesus Christ; and things that look very small to us may look very large to Christ. And when the great Christ, the Creator of heaven and earth, he who formed the heavens and the earth by his mighty power, when *he* tells of a great reward, what must it be!

Perhaps some people said to the Apostle of the Gentiles: "Now, Paul, you are meeting with too much opposition; you are suffering too much." Hear him reply, "Our light affliction, which is but for a moment, worketh for us a far more exceeding and eternal weight of glory." "Our light affliction," he said. We should have called it pretty hard, pretty heavy, should we not? But he says, "These light afflictions are nothing; think of the glory before me, and think of the crowning time; think of the reward that is laid up for me. I am on my way; the righteous Judge will give it to me when the time comes." And that is what filled his soul with joy; it was the thought of the reward that the Lord had in store for him.

Now, my friends, let us just think for a minute, think of what Paul accomplished. Think of going out, as it were, among the heathen, the first missionary, to preach to these men—who were so full of wickedness, so full of enmity and bitterness—the glorious gospel of Jesus Christ; and to tell them that the man who died outside the walls of the city of Jerusalem the death of a common prisoner, a common felon, in the sight of the world, was the promised Christ; to tell them that they had to believe in that crucified man in order to enter the kingdom of God. Think of the dark mountain that rose up before him; think of the opposition; think of the bitter persecution; and then think of the trifles in our way.

Songs in the Prison

A great many people think Paul's life was a failure. Probably his enemies, when they put him in prison, thought that would silence him. But do you know that I believe today Paul thanks God more for prisons, for stripes, for persecution, and for the opposition that he suffered, than for anything else that happened to him here? The very things we do not like are sometimes the very best for us.

Christians might not have had his glorious epistles if Paul had not been thrown into prison. It was in prison that he took up his pen and wrote those letters to the Christians in Galatia and Ephesus, in Philippi and Colosse, and to Philemon and Timothy. Look at the two epistles that he wrote to the Corinthians. How much has been done for the world by these epistles! What a blessing they have been to the church of God! How great a light they have thrown on the life of many a man! But we might not have had those epistles if it had not been for persecution.

Perhaps John Bunyan blesses God more today for Bedford jail than for anything that happened to him. Probably we would not have *Pilgrim's Progress* if he had not been thrown into that prison. Satan thought he accomplished a great deal when he shut up Bunyan there for twelve years and six months, but what a blessing it was to the world! And I believe Paul blesses God today for the imprisonment he suffered at Rome, because it gave him time to write those blessed letters. Talk of Alexander making the world tremble with the tread of his armies, and of Caesar's and Napoleon's power; but here is a little tentmaker, who, without an army, turned the world upside down.

Why? Because God Almighty was with him.

They threw Paul into prison; but it was all the same—it did not move him. When he was at Corinth and Athens preaching, it was all the same. He just pressed "toward the mark for the prize of his high calling." If God wanted him to go through prisons to win the prize, it was all the same to him. They put him in prison, but they put the Lord in with him; and Paul was so linked to Jesus that they could not separate them. He would rather be in prison with Christ than out of prison without him. He would a thousand times rather be cast into prison with the Son of God and suffer a little persecution for a few days here, than be living at ease without him.

He heard the cry, "Come over into Macedonia, and help us." He went over, and he preached; and the first thing that happened to him was that he was put into the Philippian jail. Now, if he had been as faint-hearted as most of us, he would have been disappointed and cast down. There would have been a good deal of complaining. He would have said, "This is a strange providence; what brought me here? I thought the Lord called me here. Here I am in prison in a strange city; how did I ever get here? How shall I ever get out of this place? I have no money; I have no friends; I have no attorney; I have no one to intercede for me—and here I am."

Paul and Silas were not only in prison, but their feet were made in fast in the stocks. There they were, in the inner prison, the inner dungeon—a dark, cold, damp dungeon. But at midnight the prisoners heard a strange sound. They had never heard anything like it before. They heard singing. I do not know what song those two imprisoned evangelists sang; but I know one thing, it was not a doleful sound from the tombs. You know we have a hymn: "Hark, from the tombs a doleful sound!" They did not sing that; but the Bible tells us they sang praises. A prison was a strange place to sing praises in, was it not?

I suppose it was time for the evening prayers, and that they had just had their evening prayer and then sang their evening song. And God answered their prayers; and the old prison shook, and the chains fell off, and the prison doors were opened. Yes! Yes! I have no doubt that in the glory Paul thanks God that he went to jail and that the Philippian jailer became converted.

Swept into Heaven

Then look at Paul in Rome. Nero has signed his death warrant. Take your stand, and mark that little man. He is small; in the sight of the world he is "contemptible." The world frowns upon him. Go to the palace of the king, and talk about that criminal—about Paul—and you will see a sneer on their countenances.

"Oh, he is a fanatic," they say; "he has gone mad." I wish the world was filled with such madmen. I tell you—what we need today are a few madmen like him; men who fear nothing but sin, and love nothing but God.

Rome had never had such a conqueror within its walls. Rome had never had such a mighty man as Paul within its boundaries. Although the world looked down upon him, and he perhaps appeared very small and contemptible; yet in the sight of heaven he was the mightiest man who ever trod the streets of Rome. Probably there will never be another one like him traveling over those streets. The Son of God walked with him. And go into that prison; there he is: officials come to him, and tell him that Nero has signed his death warrant. Paul does not tremble; he is not afraid.

"Paul, are you not sorry you have been so zealous for Christ? It is going to cost you your life. If you had to live your life over again, would you give it to Jesus of Nazareth?" What do you think the old warrior would reply? See those eyes light up as he replies: "If I had ten thousand lives I would give every one of those lives to Christ. The only regret I have is that I did not commence earlier and serve him better; the only regret I have now is that I ever lifted my voice against Jesus of Nazareth."

"But they are going to behead you." "Well, they may take my head, but the Lord has my heart: I care nothing about my head. The Lord has my heart, and has had it for years; they cannot separate me from the Lord. And when my head is taken off, I shall depart to be with Christ, which is far better."

They led him out. I do not know at what hour; perhaps it was early in the morning. There is a tradition that they led him two miles out of the city. Look at the little tentmaker as he goes along through the streets of Rome with a firm tread. Look at that giant as he moves through the streets. He is on his way to execution. Take your stand by his side, and hear him talk. He is speaking of the glory beyond.

He says: "Henceforth there is laid up for me a crown of righteousness. I shall see the King in his beauty tonight. I have longed to be with him. I have longed to see him. This is the day of my crowning."

The world pitied him; but he did not need its pity. He had something the world did not have. Burning within him he had a love and zeal which the world knew nothing about. Ah, the love that Paul had for Jesus Christ! But oh, the greater love the Lord Jesus had for Paul!

The hour had come. The way they used to behead in those days was for the prisoner to bend his head, when a Roman soldier would take a sharp sword and cut it off. The hour had come; and I seem to see Paul, with a joyful countenance, bending that blessed head of his; and the soldier's sword came down and set his spirit free.

If our eyes could look as Elisha's looked, we might have seen him leap into a chariot of light like Elijah; we might have seen him go sweeping upward through limitless space. Look at him now as he mounts higher and higher—look at him! See him move up! up! up! ever upward! Look at him yonder!

See! He is entering now the Eternal City of the glorified saints, the blissful abode of the Savior's redeemed ones. The prize he so long sought is at hand. See the gates yonder—how they fly wide open! See the herald angels yonder on the shining battlements of heaven. Hear the glad shouts that are passed along, "He is coming!" "He is coming!"

And he goes sweeping through the pearly gates, up along the shining way, to the very throne of God; and Christ stands there and says, "Well done, good and faithful servant! Enter thou into the joy of thy Lord."

Just think of hearing the Master say that! It will be reward enough.

O friends, your turn and mine will come by and by, if we are but faithful. Let us see that we do not lose the crown. Let us awake and put on the whole armor of God. Let us press forward into the conflict—for it is a glorious privilege. Then to us too, as to the glorified of old, will come that blessed welcome into heaven: "Well done, thou good and faithful servant!"

Further Reading

Bradford, Gamaliel. *D. L. Moody: A Worker in Souls.* Garden City: Doubleday, Doran, 1928.

Christian History 25 (9, 1990).

Daniels, W. H. *D. L. Moody and His Work.* Hartford: American Publishing Co., 1875.

Dorsett, Lyle W. *A Passion for Souls: The Life of D. L. Moody.* Chicago: Moody, 1997.

Findlay, James F. Jr. *Dwight L. Moody: American Evangelist, 1837–1899.* Chicago: University of Chicago Press, 1969.

Fitt, Arthur P. *A Shorter Life of D. L. Moody.* Chicago: Bible Institute Colportage Association, 1900.

Gundry, Stanley N. *Love Them In: The Life and Theology of D. L. Moody.* 1976. Reprint. Grand Rapids: Baker, 1982.

Moody, Paul. *My Father: An Intimate Portrait of Dwight L. Moody.* Boston: Little, Brown, 1938.

Moody, William R. *The Life of Dwight L. Moody.* Chicago: Revell, 1900.

______. *D. L. Moody.* New York: Macmillan, 1930.

Pollock, John C. *Moody: A Biography.* 1984. Reprint. Grand Rapids: Baker, 1997. Previously issued as *Moody: A Biographical Portrait of the Pacesetter in Modern Mass Evangelism.* Grand Rapids: Zondervan, 1963.

Rost, Stephen. *Dwight L. Moody: The Best from All His Works.* Nashville: Thomas Nelson, 1989.

Smith, Wilbur M. *Dwight Lyman Moody: An Annotated Bibliography*. Chicago: Moody, 1948.

______, ed. *The Best of D. L. Moody*. Chicago: Moody, 1971.

Turnbull, Ralph, ed. *The Best of Dwight L. Moody*. Grand Rapids: Baker, 1971.